TALES OF
THE OLD WATERLOO

by Allan Barham

In the 1960's a family struggles to re-open a derelict hotel in North Wales, aided and abetted by some amazing eccentrics.

"It's all gone now. The old place has been pulled down and today a new hotel stands in its place. Both my parents are dead, old Bob too and most of the others. Like the tourists, we at the Waterloo also bounced off the window of village life without leaving a mark, and now as you pass the spot you would never know that it had all happened …. But it did."

Published in Gt. Britain in 2000 by
Toby Books
P.O. Box No. 1274
Conway
LL32 8ZD

ISBN 0 95357 16 0 2

Printed and bound in Gt. Britain by
Deanprint Ltd
Stockport
Cheshire

Published in 2000

CONTENTS

CHAPTER 1

When my father bought the Waterloo Hotel in 1962, its elegant interior was crumbling fast and clearly its time was coming to an end, but what a last few years we gave the place … and what a time it gave us.

It was a massive grey stone building that stood alongside the London to Holyhead road in the village of Betws-y-Coed in North Wales. It had grown bit by bit from a small coaching inn to become a rambling architectural Frankenstein, a towering landmark of over a hundred rooms that had outlived its place in high society long before the start of the Second World War, but the Waterloo had a life of its own, it lived. It was a monster, and yet in some ways it was perhaps more like an old fruit tree, gnarled and withered and at the end of its life, it awoke and blossomed again as fruit trees sometimes do before crashing to the ground.

There's nothing of it left now except for a few outbuildings hidden behind the modern hotel someone's built in its place. When it was sold the new owners brought along a crane with an iron ball swinging on the end of a chain, and completely destroyed it.

It came down in no time, the upper floors crashing straight through taking all beneath them to the cellars below, and there in the rubble and the clouds of dust was buried once and for all my father's belief that dry rot could be killed by blue paint. As with the birth of many family businesses I expect, our investment wasn't so much in cash but commitment, and those of us who lived and ate on the premises worked for no more than pocket money. It was all for the future, the start of a dynasty, and members of the family passed in and out of it like actors in a farce, some never to be seen again.

Buying the Waterloo was a dream come true for my father, the grasping of a life-long and wild ambition. This very intelligent and normally level headed man first decided to buy the place when still very young. In those days in the early 1930's it was still a 'grand' hotel with a uniformed doorman always on duty and always a line of Rolls Royces in the kerb, and the day my father, Cyril William Barham, made up his mind to have it, he too was in the kerb.

To be precise he was on a motorbike and having found that lunch there was rather more than he could afford, he leaned over to my mother sitting in the side-car and said, "I'll buy this place for you one day."

It's not clear whether this was due to wounded pride or an early profit-motivated form of 'love at first sight', but either way it was a strange thing for a young Process Engraver from the East End of London to say.

Nevertheless, a few years later, he returned from the war to pick himself up and bury the bombed out remains of a highly successful business he'd established in the city, and after gaining a foothold in the tourist industry in Colwyn Bay and Llandudno, he was eventually able to meet his Waterloo.

It had been empty for years and in the end those selling were happy to let it go at any price. It was in a terrible state. Everyone who saw it said it was a ruin, the whole family, everyone, and of course they were the bravest, the ones who dared to walk into it. My father however thought it was wonderful. With no more than a few weeks spent patching it up he was ready to take up the curtain, and he was so sure of success he persuaded everyone to join the cast, even me.

Like pot-holers we groped our way by torchlight through the evil smelling cellars in those first full days of exploration. Sid, Ron and I trailing in the smoky wake of my father's pipe, over piles of debris, coke, and rats both dead and alive, following the course of great rusty iron water pipes to their long lost source at an enormous boiler, and up in the lofts we crawled warily beneath the slates through curtains of thick acrid smoke-blackened cobwebs, over wet and sagging rafters green with rot, replacing countless generations of rusted buckets, bowls and tin cans with more buckets, bowls and tin cans to catch the rain as it splattered in with shafts of misty daylight, tinted like rainbows.

Most of the stately rooms beneath, which for years had offered the best in affluent accommodation to the travellers of the world, including foreign Royalty according to a mouldy old visitors book, now had gaping holes in the ceilings and the crumbled horse hair plaster lay beneath the naked laths in piles on bare and filthy floors. Paper hung peeling from the walls and dry rot fungus sprouted like mushrooms and pancakes from the skirting boards.

I don't know where my father got all that blue paint, but its effect was short lived.

It all took off with so much optimism and now it's all gone. So often I wish there was something, a keepsake or a relic, something that we could have salvaged from that era, and looking back as I do a great deal these days, I suppose there was one thing we could have tried to save long before the end came. Something that long before our arrival had been an important part of the hotel's early prosperity, but it's too late now.

When I was up in that part of the forest recently alongside the pounding white falls of the Lledr, I saw no trace of it. A wet mist from the deafening torrent was slowly drifting through the trees but even in that gloom, if a single shaft or rusting iron step from that old horse drawn coach had survived, I think I would have seen it.

When first I saw it there many, many years ago, it was falling apart even then, but the words 'The Waterloo Hotel' were still visible on the doors. I was a boy then of about twelve or thirteen, a bare kneed boy-scout from Colwyn Bay camping on a farm up in the back woods of the Lledr Valley. Four of us, picking our way along the bank over mossy rocks with worms dangling from rods and sticks, stumbled across it in amazement, and soon we were pretending to be driving it, whipping up the horses and fighting off highwaymen and hordes of Indians for good measure with all thought of fishing gone for the day.

I'm not even sure if it was standing on its wheels, but the seats had been ripped from it and remnants of mouldy blue material hung in shreds from its gaping windows. There was no telling how it had got down there into that wood but even then the name of the hotel it had so obviously served, meant something to me. I knew it was the hotel my father had always wanted to own, and just ten years later he at last bought it, and the Waterloo became my home for five years.

It never occurred to me though, as we fought to breathe life back into the hotel, to try and retrieve what might have been left of the old coach, which is strange perhaps because as we got stuck into all that plastering, painting and papering, one of the first legends we learnt about this

5

'gold mine' village we'd moved into, involved the Waterloo's coachman.

In the days between the stage coach and the motor car, Betws-y-Coed's fame as a tourist trap was forged by the steam-engine. When the branch line of the railway was brought up the Conway Valley during the 1860's, the hotels sent horse drawn carriages rattling into the station yard to meet the trains and tout for business.

According to local legend the Waterloo employed a coachman, who being paid no doubt on commission, made full use of the Swallow Falls to fill his coach.

There's no exact record of his patter, but it seems he was enormously successful in luring arrivals into his coach by shouting, "Come and stay at the Waterloo, the hotel with the best views across to the world famous Swallow Falls."

It's true that the Swallow Falls were indeed becoming in those early days of tourism, very famous, but a glance at any map of the area will show that while the Waterloo was pleasantly situated on the banks of the River Conway half a mile to the east of the railway station, the Swallow Falls were, and still are to this day, two miles to the west of the railway station and on a different river altogether.

The waterfall that he pointed out to them was no more than a modest splash of water, no different from dozens of similar streams that plunge down from the woods into the River Conway. It's there to this day, close to the eastern side of the Waterloo Bridge.

I often used to think of that old coachman as we took up the struggle to capture the all important customers, to rope in enough of them to make a living in that gaunt stone fortress, nailing up huge signboards on tottering posts, and plastering the windows with ghastly orange posters proclaiming that bed and breakfast was only 17/6, or as we would say today 87½p.

Without the pressure, without the constant struggle to pay people and to keep out of debt, it's easy now to shudder at what we did there to improve access and bring in more people. The felling of the great oaks, the ripping down of the sombre ivy that had graced the walls for generations, mostly on the outside of the building, the smashing down of the great glass porch, the covering of an acre size lawn with tarmac that immediately became a dusty litter strewn eyesore, the opening of a rubbish fast food snack bar, the liberal and hideous splashwork of job-lot blue paint on every window frame, and the building of a filling station that filled the whole place with diesel fumes, but never once in those mad days when both the building and my father were entering their last chapter, did we ever see it as a disaster. Perhaps it didn't last long enough for that.

In those five short years, we really should have done

something about buying that old coach back, no matter how dilapidated, it would have stood as a memorial to us all, but especially to two men. A long time separated them, they never met, but they came from that same mould of pure optimism. One was my father who worried about nothing if he could fix it for the time being with a six inch nail, and the other was the old coachman.

Whoever that old boy was I came to admire him enormously. He must have been quite a character. You have to admire a man who had the nerve to tell a coach load of well informed Victorians that the humble splash of water just visible across the river was the most famous waterfall in Great Britain, a national landmark of Her Majesty's realm that was currently being painted in oils and graphically described by practically every leading artist and travel writer of the day!

How long his deception went on for I cannot say, but the rogue may well have paid for it at the hands of his competitors. This story fails to name the victim, but apparently a sleeping coachman awoke on the arrival of a train one day to find no one coming to his coach. His patter was in vain and when he returned without a single customer, it was revealed that during his sleep in the station yard, rival coachmen from other hotels had climbed up to him and quietly painted his face with the one thing Victorians were terrified of, an enormous rash of highly contagious looking spots.

My father paid a much higher price for his audacity. The story ended when he dropped dead. In the Spring of 1966 at the age of 56 he had a stroke.

If his qualities were optimism and perseverance it must also be said that he had no idea of running a hotel. He ran it as no more than a boozer with bedrooms, but he loved the place – he loved the life and the friends he made there, but as a hotel it was a shambles. Even for special functions, weddings or special dinners it was always a case of 'make do somehow'. Anyone asking in advance for guaranteed standards, like a menu, was usually persuaded to forget it.

He'd got what he had set his heart on and apart from hanging onto it nothing else mattered, and now this man of very old fashioned morals, who'd been very nearly tee-total, who didn't like rude jokes, and never swore, who'd never suffered fools gladly, and who'd never mixed willingly outside the family circle, was host at the noisiest, rowdiest pub it's possible to imagine.

For the first time since being in the army he'd found an abundance of good down-to-earth friends among the boozers of that village. This was the new family circle, and he couldn't step out of that circle, and strangers looking for something out of the ordinary like a bath or a dinner were a damn nuisance.

One year I persuaded him to accept an offer that I thought was going to be the making of us. The RAC wanted us to provide all the accommodation, the catering, the booze, the petrol and servicing area as the overnight headquarters of the RAC Rally as it swept through Wales. In the end he agreed, and after the GPO had installed a battery of extra telephones, the whole circus arrived, attended by hundreds of spectators, all the famous competitors, back-up teams, officials and journalists from all over the world, and eventually as dawn broke and the last of the mud splattered cars had roared off up the road, and my father had counted up the considerable takings for the night, he went to bed saying "Good riddance."

In his opinion they had all been hangers on and parasites and it wasn't long before he banned all coach parties, even when an orchestra walked in one day – I think it was the BBC Symphony Orchestra, but he wouldn't serve them, he said they were all a bunch of long-haired louts.

"Get out," he said, "You're making the place look untidy."

We never had a chef. After breakfast if my mother or her sister couldn't get back in the kitchen because of innumerable other problems, a couple of cleaners would cook the lunches. Even I made Yorkshire puddings between serving petrol, trying hard to keep the oily thumb prints firmly on the *outside* of the bowl.

On the whole, my father's total lack of planning was a model for the approaching age of industrial flexibility. He spent every day running from one end of the building to the other in a cloud of blue smoke from his pipe, usually passing my mother at the half way point going in the opposite direction.

This was mainly due to the fact that he wisely decided to scrap the filthy pre-war kitchen at the back and equip a new one. A new one, I should add, at either end of the building. One was a kitchen for the snack bar we built with scraps of rough wood and off-cuts of red and yellow Formica, in what had been a very nice lounge, and at the other end of the vast building we used a couple of spare rooms to make a kitchen for what he called proper meals, for lunches and residents breakfasts.

This situation was further complicated when he equipped a third kitchen somewhere in the middle to use when a smaller dining room came into use, when the large dining room wasn't busy enough!

It was nothing more than an asylum, and every day apart from the culinary chaos there were always running repairs to do in the bedrooms. To cure the problem of lost keys he made it so that all bedroom keys fitted all bedroom doors. Guests thought they had the key to their door, but actually *all* the keys fitted *all* the doors, but there were still

11

problems. The doors fell off! Sinks got blocked, beds collapsed, ceilings collapsed, and adding to the structural mayhem was the staff.

Some of them of course were other hotel's rejects and there were some who daily stole anything weighing under two-hundredweight and not actually nailed down, but they weren't all dishonest. Others had more interesting problems. There was the cleaning lady who had to be reminded to plug in the vacuum cleaner. Electricity is a wonderful thing, but we had to agree that pushing the thing around without plugging it in was much quieter, and there was the cook who might have become a real cook (in time) had she been able to light the electric cooker. She went once she'd run out of matches. I don't know if she'd seen an electric cooker before, but time and time again that morning, she tried to light it with a match. The box was empty by lunchtime and we never saw her again.

Acquiring people who were reliable was one thing, but keeping them of course was another thing altogether. Cleaners especially were a problem.

Several left because they said it was too old to clean, several left because it was too *cold* to clean, and others left because they said they were frightened of spiders. Two in particular claimed to have seen an enormous spider that was so big it chased them, one round a bedroom and the other down the stairs.

My father didn't believe them of course, but rumours spread and the mythical spider became something of a legend, and he was no more sympathetic with those who claimed to have been frightened by phantom footsteps, but I believed them alright. The place was full of queer noises.

Waitresses too were a problem. There were waitresses who got too drunk to walk between the tables, and waitresses who disappeared into the linen room to kiss and cuddle with anyone they picked up in the bar.

All meal times were a farce as far as service was concerned. Breakfast, lunch or dinner it didn't matter, the dining room was more like a market place. While waitresses gathered in groups gossiping, the milkman, the butcher and the grocer would push through the tables to deliver their goods to the kitchens. No one used the tradesmen's entrance. Black with coal dust, the coal-men would come in to check the stockpile in the cellars and stop for a cuppa, chatting to the diners, and there was always a poacher or two coming in to wander around the tables selling salmon.

I think the guests liked all this street life, those that stayed for a second night anyway. Especially when they could take home a salmon for what today would be 30p a lb., and wandering around in the middle of it all of course was a 'tramp' in hob nail boots – our handy-man Bob, who had an enormously loud and hearty greeting for absolutely everyone, guests included.

Old Bob had the happy but totally mystifying knack of being able to get drunk every morning simply by stocking up the bar. My mother, who was a very patient and understanding little woman, used all her persuasive charms to cure him, shouting at him and hitting him, but it made no difference. Bob was with us from the start. God knows how we got him, but at least he was one of the few that wasn't a reject from one of the other hotels.

He was a reject from the Forestry Commission, apparently for blowing up a tree.

This old bachelor, who spent most of his days either laughing or crying, was reckoned to be a dab-hand with the dynamite, especially when he was sober, but the last straw came when he was asked to remove a tree. They'd been making a new road through the forest and he removed it with dynamite. The extra sticks he stuffed into it for good measure, rained too many pieces of tree onto too many important people over too great an area for any more last chances, so he decided to help us instead.

It was the beginning of the end of old Bob too. He died soon after my father. They made a great pair in those last few years of their lives. When my father died, old Bob cried for two whole days.

"What are we going to do?" he kept asking, "What are we going to do?"

When we sold up in 1967, he thought no one else would take him on but thank goodness someone did.

The Betws-y-Coed UDC was said to be the smallest Urban District Council in the land. They had a number of public buildings and an estate of council houses to maintain, but they didn't have any sort of motor vehicle. All they had was a wheelbarrow and Bob became the new wheelbarrow man. Heaven knows what chaos that must have caused.

When we had embarked on re-opening the Old Waterloo though, back in those fresh new days of optimism, we had needed all the help we could get, and Bob came along. If only we had realised. If only we had known we were going to get it from someone like Bob.

One Christmas before joining us he'd cooked himself an oven-ready frozen duck. When it came out of the oven it was far from being a success. It smelt awful and looked even worse, and puzzled by this he went and brought the grocer from his Christmas lunch to have a look at it. He wasn't very pleased of course to be dragged away from the dinner table. Especially when he found the duck was still in its plastic wrapper.

CHAPTER 2

It's strange really but in spite of my father's determined individualism and all that he instilled within us, it was the locals, the people who worked for us, the visitors, and most of all the place itself that really made the stories I have to tell.

I can only say that my father brought them all together, but once the furniture lorries had dropped their loads from warehouses and auction rooms, the draymen had rolled in the first lot of barrels and the frozen chips had arrived, and at last we had hung up the 'open' signs and the Waterloo's heart was beating again, it was by then, out of his hands. The old place just took over our lives.

oooooOooooo

The night Bob promised to help with the concreting was like any other head splitting Summer night at the Waterloo, which for some reason had become the singing pub for the whole area. Every night the enormous crescendo of beery voices raised in song rocked the old place to its foundations with a non-stop combination of bawdy songs and really passionate hymns, a speciality they claim of Welshmen everywhere.

Until long after closing time, a densely packed crowd of tourists pressed in hard upon the locals, from the front doors they pressed in through the pink pillared arches of the reception area in the front bar, through to the back room where Dai Bradley's hammering on the upright piano in that smoky haze, was no more than a mime, the sound of it completely lost in a continual deafening chorus.

On that night when at last the singing dissolved into closing time applause, old Bob in an effort to stop the world spinning, clapped his hands upon my shoulders.

For a while, with the applause going on and on, he searched not only for words, but for me too as he tried to focus his vision, his watery blue eyes totally glazed, as usual.

His predicament was resolved eventually by my mother. Shouting into my ear as loud as she could from only six inches away, she told me it was his birthday, which at least was a new excuse.

Giving up the struggle to see straight he began instead a long exaggerated wink to emphasise the solemnity of what he was about to say. "In the morning I'll be here" he said at last with enormous sincerity. "I won' let you down."

I tried to tell him we'd manage. "It's your day off tomorrow Bob, you have a lie in" I said but it was to no avail.

"I wan' to help," he insisted, "I won' let you down Nox."

He called a lot of his mates Nox for some reason, and with that last assurance he was swept out the door by the fast flowing human tide, one hand aloft, the other struggling to pull his cap on.

Bob's transport was an old black bike, probably as old as he was, and somehow or other he must have got it home that night because he turned up on it the next day, but not as promised in the morning.

The building of the petrol station at the snack bar end of the hotel was at an important stage. The car park tarmac had been spread all over the lawns and a huge and very deep pit had been dug close to the petrol pumps. The excavating machine had left the site and four big fuel tanks had been lowered into the hole to await the concrete that would bury them, but that day we were working on another area of concrete. We were making the forecourt, an area of concrete around the pump island, a long narrow, slightly raised traffic island, rounded either end like a boat on which the petrol pumps stood. The four pumps stood in a row with a little kiosk in the middle. It was very small by today's standards, but the area either side of the pump island took a lot of concrete and it came in a fleet of ready-mix lorries throughout the afternoon. It was about 4 o'clock when we finally finished smoothing it over with

spades and a long plank of wood that we'd shunted to and
fro across each wet and gleaming section. I suppose it was
about twelve inches deep and it looked really good. It
certainly looked as if some hard work had gone into it.

Bob arrived as the last ready-mix lorry was preparing
to leave. The driver had folded back the chute behind the
great revolving drum and was now engaged with last
minute fastenings, when suddenly from the road there
came the sound of motor horns and the screeching of
brakes.

As we looked up to see what the commotion was about,
the traffic was coming to a stop. At first our view was
blocked by several dozen vehicles, their exhausts fuming
indignantly, but instinctively I knew it had something to
do with Bob. Perhaps my inkling had something to do
with the sound of a bicycle bell bouncing down the road,
I don't know, but when the traffic started to move again,
it revealed Bob standing on the white line with one leg
through the frame of his bike, shouting apologies to
passers-by, while trying to straighten out his handle bars.

The traffic moved on, avoiding him like the plague with
windows hurriedly being wound up, and soon after re-
mounting with a dozen or more hops, he swerved across
the road in front of a cattle wagon, singing his head off,
and shot across the car park towards us, crashing to a halt
against the back of the concrete lorry.

"I said I'd come and help," he cried triumphantly, grabbing the driver's lapels as the bike fell around his ankles.

The driver looked at me in silence, his face totally blank. I didn't bother to introduce them.

"We've finished Bob," I said "We've done it."

"Well," he said in amazement, staggering across to the edge of the concrete lake. "Well well," he was saying.

He was on the brink, tottering, gazing at it with bleary-eyed admiration.

"Swonderful Nox," he was saying. "Thas marvellous."

"Don't touch it Bob," I warned, as he stooped for a shovel.

I was wasting my breath. I won't beat about the bush, he fell on the wet concrete. 'Splotch' right into it.

I wish I could say he was unlucky, that he tripped over the dog or somebody threw him in, but no, the simple truth of the matter is that while I was signing the driver's delivery note, Bob entered into a losing battle with the shovel, having seen a bit that he thought needed smoothing over, he teetered on the edge, and fell in.

We rushed over but before we could pull him from it, he was rolling in it, trying of course to get up, and in a few moments he was covered in concrete. He was in a terrible mess, and when the driver and I pulled him out he lay groaning like an exhausted grey seal left behind by the

21

tide… calling for a taxi.

He was still calling for John Evans taxi when at last we got him to his feet and tried to walk him to the snack bar, but no, he just wanted to go home. Being so wet he was enormously heavy. He was so heavy we dropped him twice, and we were getting covered in concrete too.

"I wanner go 'ome," he was saying, "I wanner go 'ome Nox," and nothing could change his mind, so I went for the van, and then with the back doors wide open, we hauled him in, laid him out on the floor, dumped his bike on top of him, and I took him home.

It only took a few minutes and soon I was struggling up the garden path with him, and it was so typical of him, during those few moments in the van he'd recovered from the shock and now he couldn't stop laughing. He lived right on the main road in the centre of the village and passing tourists must have thought we were both drunk as we collapsed in a heap at the door.

Like the old Waterloo, Bob's cottage has completely disappeared now. No-one lived in it after he died and to be honest I don't know how he lived in it either. Perhaps there was nothing really wrong with the cottage itself, but the junk that was piled into it had to be seen to be believed. Cardboard boxes climbed like sky-scrapers to the ceiling alongside mountains of logs, and everywhere there were pieces of bike, picks and shovels, even rolls of barbed wire and discarded clothing.

The place was so full, the door would only just open wide enough to squeeze through and when I got him in, all he wanted to do was slump down in his armchair by the fire.

"For goodness sake Bob," I said "You can't sit there, you're covered in concrete." But he only laughed all the more.

"I'll be alright Nox," he said and stretched out his legs kicking a space for his hob-nail boots among the pokers and assorted logs and choppers in the hearth. "I'll be alright," he said repeatedly, tears rolling down his cheeks. "I'll be alright," and as I left he was singing.

ooooo**O**ooooo

A few days later the great pit was filled with masses of slushy concrete by the same fleet of ready-mix lorries that had covered the forecourt, but to fill that great hole and completely cover the fuel tanks it took all day. There were wide gaps between the tanks and all the way around the edges too, and it was very deep.

I had a couple of lads helping me that day and we were pretty pleased with ourselves by the time the last ready-mix lorry had come and gone and we'd finished smoothing that lot over.

All day we'd kept Bob well away from it. I can't remember what he was doing. Stocking up the bar I expect. We could hear him singing.

That night the old place shook to the same weight of numbers and the same noise as usual, and as usual old Bob was among the last to go, staggering out the side door where he always left his bike.

We'd just finished clearing away the glasses when the dogs started barking. They were barking and scratching away at that side door quite furiously, and when we opened it they rushed off into the darkness towards the petrol station, and immediately of course we heard him. It was Bob shouting for help like a ship-wrecked mariner. He'd cycled into the pit. He'd collided with the barrier we'd put around it, gone over the handlebars, and now he was up to his neck in concrete again and going down for the last time. It was like quicksand.

We rushed over and pulled him out, only this time with an even greater struggle, and I went for the van again. He looked such a sorry sight, especially when he put his cap on and it all ran down his face again. My father was all for getting the hosepipe but no, all he wanted to do was to go home and so I took him home and once again he collapsed into his armchair.

The next morning there was no sign of him. By 10 o'clock my father thought I ought to go and see if he was alright.

He was of course. It was a lovely morning and as I approached, I could hear him singing at the top of his voice. I don't know what it was. I don't suppose I knew at the time, but it had the same sort of rhythm and accompaniment as the anvil chorus. The words, totally indistinguishable, were punctuated by the ringing sound of a hammer hitting something hard.

I pushed the door open and there he was still in his armchair, a weird grey figure just like a stone statue that had come to life. He was bent forward smashing the concrete off his legs with a hammer and chisel.

"Come in Nox" he shouted, "I fell asleep!"

CHAPTER 3

The little red mini coming carefully down the A5 hill towards Betws-y-Coed belonged to a Londoner, a little man of quiet reputation by the name of Arthur Quinton. Beside him sat his wife and in the back their teenage daughter. Her parents were as excited as she was. After years of toil they had bought a car and this was their first real holiday.

They had no idea what they were coming to, they'd left home that morning and had simply driven north into unexplored territory. The A5 from London goes through North Wales and they were still on it at 4 o'clock in the afternoon.

As the Christmas Trees of the Gwydir Forest drifted passed on either side they watched with a feeling of enchantment. At the bottom of the hill they slowly approached the Waterloo Bridge, the graceful iron structure that was built over the river Conway in the year of the great battle, and there, a set of signposts gave them an unexpected choice.

The driver adjusted his glasses and peered ahead, the car slowing down even further. To the left the road swung out over the bridge bound for Bangor and Holyhead, while straight on the A470 offered to take them to places called

Llanrwst and Llandudno.

"Llandudno," they said together in surprise.

"That's the seaside ain' it?" a bright little voice said hopefully in the back, and at that moment with the driver's hand upon the gear stick, their fate hung in the balance.

It apparently hung there for no more than a few seconds, but as the car came to a stop, it happened.

From where it had been lurking, a huge figure sprang from the shadows and in one leap ripped open the near side door.

"Goin' to Llanrwst!" the figure bellowed at the top of its voice, head and shoulders right in on top of them and squinting at them at point blank range through glasses as thick as milk bottle bottoms.

Absolutely stunned, the occupants of the mini squirmed back in their seats, shook their heads and squeaked that they weren't, and with the stick rammed into the first forward gear it could find, the little car lurched ahead sending the intruder stumbling out backwards.

As they accelerated over the Waterloo Bridge and round the next bend they saw somewhere to hide and recover. The Waterloo Hotel – B&B 17/6.

As was often the case, I was the receptionist that afternoon for a while depending on who hadn't turned up that day. Not a job I was well suited for, but these people bursting in to explain that they'd been attacked, didn't even notice my greasy petrol station overalls.

"She wanted a lift," the woman was saying, "It was definitely a her wasn't it Arthur?"

He nodded, "yes dear."

"She thought we were going to the coast," she went on, "we nearly died. God she just ran out into the middle of the road and tried to climb in on top of us. She was terrifying."

The account went on and on and by the time we'd got up to the first landing, I couldn't help wondering if they'd ever seen our waitresses.

"She was from a lunatic asylum," the woman said emphatically, "she was definitely a lunatic, there's no doubt about that. My husband screamed when she tore open the door."

"I didn't scream dear."

"Arthur: you screamed."

"Well, I was shocked."

"You were terrified Arthur, and so was I. We saw this place and drove straight in, we were shaken, believe me we were shaken."

By then we had arrived at a couple of vacant rooms. I put the teenage miss into a single room and her parents into the one next door, room number 8.

The rest of the day went quite smoothly. Out at the petrol station Bob had gone a whole hour without getting confused over the difference between petrol and diesel and in the snack bar none of the usual troublemakers had put salt in the sugar bowls, and the customers too had been unusually courteous, some of them waving as they drove off.

When four lads in a battered Morris booked in for the night though I predicted trouble. They looked OK, but it was the way they snubbed Cortina Lil that threatened a bust up.

She was a bit of a mystery was Cortina Lil. She was very attractive. She used to appear from time to time and she had this highly polished Cortina which in those parts was a prize indeed, and when she cruised onto the car park and plonked her rear end onto a bar stool, males were required to come hither.

I was in the bar by then, behind the counter, but the four lads were sitting ducks. They bought her a couple of gins and by the time I'd worked out in which order she was going to take them, they let her down flat.

"Where's the nearest dance hall?" they asked.

"Who wants to dance?" she asked with a grin.

"Where's the nearest dance hall?" one of them asked again, only this time addressing the question to me, ignoring her completely.

"Llandudno," I said, "there's nothing here till the weekend."

"How far's that?" they wanted to know, and when I told them about twenty miles they wanted to know if they could have a key.

I had to laugh. "What do you think this place is?" I said, "a hotel? The old man doesn't believe in keys only bolts. When he goes to bed he bolts the door and anyone who's out, stays out."

Cortina Lil uncrossed her legs and then crossed them again, inching up her skirt in the process.

I felt sorry for them. In those days before the breathalyser she could drink every one of them under the table. It could cost them a fortune.

I explained it was usually one o'clock in the morning before we got cleared up in the bar so they had until then, and as long as it wasn't later than half past I'd come down if necessary and let them in.

"I usually read for about half an hour," I told them, and taking them out into the road I showed them my window.

It was a free house and the place was by then festooned with numerous brewery signs and I explained that my window was to the left of the "Red Barrel" sign.

"Don't make a row though," I warned them, "or you'll wake everybody up. Just throw a couple of pebbles up at the glass, I'll hear you."

Back in the front bar they finished their pints and off they went to the car park, searching between them for the

31

car keys.

As no more than an after thought one of them turned to the girl and said "Goodnight miss."

When Cortina Lil slid off her stool and strode after them she wore the sort of look on her face that suggested she might be going to slash their tyres.

Things by then were beginning to warm up, more customers were filtering in, my mother and her sister were upstairs dolling themselves up to appear before their "public" and Sid was stoking up the fires.

We always had a couple of good fires blazing away even in the height of summer. They stopped the wallpaper going green.

Not that it was ever summer in that building, that multi-storey mausoleum, that high rise dungeon. It was permanently damp and permanently cold. If you couldn't get near a fire to warm up it was warmer to go outside for a bit. But for some totally inexplicable reason the old Waterloo drew people like a magnet and once it was crowded enough for people to be pressed together in a scrum, the temperature rose. As the place warmed to the sound of music, or something similar massed and vocal, it sometimes warmed up enough for the more outrageous to strip. On more than one occasion I saw gloves and scarves trampled under foot.

I remember on this particular night the singing started

around eightish, earlier than usual especially as it wasn't fire brigade night, and as always, the tourists believing they'd discovered a unique pocket of rural culture, were rewarding the locals with pints as fast as they could sing and we could rake in the cash.

Altogether it was a gloriously simple arrangement that no marketing manager could ever have devised. Our bar trade flourished upon a most enviable commercial structure that in today's jargon was self-generating and highly rewarding for all sides. The locals sang, the tourists enjoyed the satisfaction of fostering a rich seam of culture, and we took the money.

If there was a deception hidden away in this process, it was only a small one and not entirely premeditated. It was simply that the locals weren't actually the simple rustics the tourists believed them to be, or indeed wanted them to be. In reality many of the locals with the loudest voices and the most desperate thirsts were among the elite of village life. Bank Managers, Teachers, Chapel Deacons, and so on …, but the average tourist can be fooled for nights on end by what he thinks is a funny accent and the Englishman especially, never manages to grasp the significance of the classless Welsh society, where the big fish swim with the little fish quite happily in the same pond.

One local, admittedly not a born and bred local, but one

of English origin, cleverly showed how desperately tourists need natives. He used to hurry round after closing his restaurant disguised as a Scotsman. He'd stand there in kilt and sporran singing away with the rest of them, and the tourists kept him going with as many pints as he could drink, and not only him but his dog also, a dog named Trojan, who became known as McTrojan, the brown highland Labrador. Even when the 'Scotsman' swapped his pint pot for a two pint pot, the beer still flowed unabated, but then with best bitter at the equivalent to something less than 10p a pint it was all so easy.

Pete's success in showing that the tourists in their search for natives are in no way selective, led him on to further experiments. Even his appearances as an African native were rewarding, with fuzzy black wig, a face full of boot polish and sunglasses, but his sudden switch to being a Welshman was a mistake. Not that the real Welshmen objected, far from it they thought he was great, but his act was actually a little too real. He decided that like most real Welshmen he'd be a descendant of Owain Glyndwr, but when a wandering English journalist appeared on the scene looking for Welshmen of royal blood, someone gave him the name of Peter Dodd, the Welshman with the giant Corgi.

Returning however, to this particular night, apart from an earlier start than usual to the singing, it was shaping up in a pretty average sort of way. Dai, a burly forester by day and our baritone barman by night, was trying to sell Alan Atkinson, a cockney local, a horse-drawn hearse, and a Welsh teacher and his mate from Llanrwst were persuading a couple of girls from Manchester to go on a Beaver hunt, deep in the forest and after dark of course. There was a chap offering advice on the recommended wall height for a snake pit in an African Zoo, a bloke from Blaenau Ffestiniog was trying to sell some gelignite, two dozen climbers round one of the fires were hanging their socks from the mantelpiece, all the chickens roasting on the spit had had their legs stolen, and Bob had fallen off his stool.

He was sitting propped up against the piano fast asleep in spite of the noise, and amazing though it may seem, people constantly filed in off the street to ask for accommodation in that atmosphere, clambering over rucksacks, dogs and bodies and squeezing through to the bar where they had to shout to be heard, and one couple who asked for a room that night appeared to Sid at least, to be familiar.

"Haven't they been before?" he asked me, but I wasn't sure.

"*He* has," he said, "I think he's a coalman from Wrexham, but I'm not sure about her," he added as he closed the visitors book and I passed him another tray of empty glasses.

Next time I brought in another tray of glasses, Sid had definitely decided it wasn't the woman the man had been with last time.

I don't know who'd shown them up to a room, but that was the last anyone saw of them.

When I went to bed, after the nightly chore of washing up hundreds of glasses in a grimy back room sink before the rats came up through the holes in the floor to scrounge for their supper, I found the Wrexham coalman was in the room next to mine. I recognised his voice.

I was quietly unlocking my door when he burst into a fit of hysterics.

"He's coming in the door!" he shouted. "He's coming in.! He's coming in!"

Of course I wasn't doing anything of the sort, and he quite obviously had somebody else on his mind, but the problem was that the rooms had once been one large room, and at some time before our arrival on the scene it had been divided into two by a very thin partition, and the doors were very close to each other.

As I climbed into bed I could hear her calming him down and eventually I settled down too and was soon asleep.

How long I was asleep I've no idea, but I was suddenly woken up by the coalman shouting in absolute panic again.

36

"He's coming through the window! My God, he's coming through the window!"

He was going berserk. I sat up in bed and as I did so there was a cry from outside, followed a second or two later by a thud below.

I leapt out of bed, stumbled across the room and falling over shoes and a chair full of clothes, flung back the curtain.

In the next room it was still pandemonium but outside, down there in a pool of yellow light from a street lamp, someone was sprawling on his back in the flower bed wailing "ee" and "eck" and wrestling with a coil of rope.

For a moment it was like watching a cat playing with a ball of tangled wool, but suddenly like a flash he was on his feet, the rope was over his shoulder, and grabbing a bike from against the wall he furiously peddled up the road towards Capel Curig.

Heavy footsteps thudded across the room next door and the window was brought crashing down, rattling mine fit to bust in the process. Like the doors, the windows too were only narrowly divided by the partition, but as I stood there I realised there were some strange shadowy figures lurking under the tree on the far side of the road.

As I stood watching they started to wave. As quietly as I could, I pushed up my window for a clearer view. As I did so they tiptoed closer. When I put my head out of the window they started to whisper, loudly.

"For Christ sake let us in!"

Of course! I realised then who they were, they were the lads who'd gone to Llandudno. I'd forgotten all about them.

When I went down and opened the front door they said they'd tried throwing pebbles up at my window and were just deciding to sleep in the car when round the corner came a climber on a bike.

"He was broad Lancashire" one said, "he screeched to a stop and said, "What's up lads?"

"When we told him" another added, "he said 'Ee I'll get the blighter out of bed' and he pulled off his rope, lassoed the Red Barrel sign and walked straight up the wall. Unfortunately though he opened the wrong window!"

"Then all hell broke out" another said, "I think someone threw a pillow at him because he fell backwards off the window ledge and landed in the flower bed."

Next morning on my way down to the kitchen for my breakfast, I found my mother attending to the less glamorous side of the job, serving up the early morning cups of tea. She used a tiny box room above the porch as her centre of early morning tea making, and there she was, pouring out dozens of cups and arranging them on trays mostly in pairs with neatly folded paper napkins.

While Joyce started things going in the breakfast kitchen, my mother would often have to serve all the teas herself, all over the building, but this particular morning was a good one, a waitress had turned up.

My mother and I had no sooner said good morning when a shriek burst from a room at the far end of the corridor. As shrieks go it was nothing like the coalman's. It was short, and stifled quickly, like one smothered under a blanket.

As we ran out into the hall the waitress emerged from a bedroom squinting through her glasses and looking very bewildered.

"I banged on the door," she bellowed, "someone said 'come in' and when I went in he screamed."

I looked past her at the number on the bedroom door. It was number 8, the people in the red mini.

I was afraid she'd been one of ours.

CHAPTER 4

One day I took part in a fox hunt. It was as far removed from a traditional English hunt as it's possible to imagine. There was no riding in the pink upon steaming great hunters, no horns a-wailing or hounds a-baying or any such gathering of fine ladies and gentlemen partaking of the stirrup cup afore the 'tallyho'. No, here there was no sherry, no horses or dogs, and definitely no women.

This farmer's hunt was purely functional. It was said there were too many foxes in the area and some had to be shot. With this in mind one Friday night, Bob the gamekeeper asked me to help.

It was a Friday and we had a dance on, and squashed into the ballroom with a couple of hundred people dancing to a local group called 'The Saphires' –blasting out the Twist and the Hippy Hippy Shakes, it was almost impossible to hear him, but he kept on about this fox hunt and he almost made it sound like an honour to be invited.

Bob was no gamekeeper and as far as I know, never had been. He was just one more piece in the tapestry of local fantasy, and to this end he carried a shotgun and dragged a couple of terriers around the village every day. He certainly looked the part dressed as he always was in a gamekeeper's jacket and a sort of Sherlock Holmes hat, but in fact he worked for the Forestry Commission on pest control. His aim in life was to shoot a couple of grey squirrels every day, and these he seemed to think were to be found most mornings in the back bar of the Waterloo.

Strangely for an outdoor type he always looked as if he was at death's door, and you never felt you understood him fully or that he fully understood you. There seemed to be a sort of time warp running through every conversation, with comments and replies never quite synchronising.

He lived up in the forest with his elderly mother. He was a painfully shy man and I think he took to us because we made less fun of him than some of those he'd known all his life; until he got himself a horse.

That shy desire to be noticed certainly had its chance the day his horse ran off with him. He went straight through the village wrapped round its neck, and that was the last we saw of it. In fact we didn't see Bob for a fortnight.

He always wanted to be one of the local characters, but he just didn't have that vital knack of deception. When he tagged onto the other story-tellers in the bar and told the tourists about the forest and its dangers it never rang true, and when he told them about the pole-cats that would rip your throat out if you didn't get them with the first shot, they never really believed him.

He tried hard, but he had neither the bravado of the really great liars or anything of the 'dead pan' approach of someone like Don the postman.

One night in the height of summer, with the bar full of holidaymakers, Don the postman arrived on a bicycle dressed as a chapel minister in a shabby black suit, dog collar and black hat, and with a perfectly straight face he cycled through the front door between dozens of total strangers and after dismounting leant his bike against the bar. All the chatter died instantly and the tourists looked on in silence as Dai behind the bar responded without batting an eyelid, and carefully filled the basket on the handlebars with bottles of whisky and gin.

No one knew what to make of it and soon some were beginning to giggle, but all the postman did was look at them solemnly while he studiously poked a finger through his broken spectacles and rubbed an eye. For some that did it and the place was instantly in an uproar. There were people literally bent double in agony, and as he mounted his bike he seriously told them he was only stocking up for the week and he didn't expect to be laughed at, and with that he rode out the door.

There were numerous lunatics at large like that and some used to scare the tourists to death, old Ellis Hughes for instance who'd split his sides asking any woman with a purse if she'd marry him.

He was a ruddy-faced old farmer who lived alone up in the Lledr Valley and he used to arrive on a horse and cart. There was no conceit about Ellis Hughes, I've seen smarter scarecrows. Like old Bob, if he had a Sunday Best we never saw it at the Waterloo, but this King of characters couldn't give a damn, and when he tied his horse to the railings you could hear him as soon as he came through the door, a burst of cackling laughter that deteriorated into an asthmatic wheeze and a spluttering death rattle by chucking out time.

He certainly did all he could to enjoy himself and I've seen women of all ages run for their lives when he walked in with his arms wide open, and always he had an indestructible old brown dog-end glued to his bottom lip, the only thing visible in that big apparently toothless wet mouth. He couldn't help it but he drenched you every time he spoke to you, and it didn't matter who she was or who she was with, if he thought a woman in the bar had some cash he'd offer to take her down the isle.

After he'd laughed himself to exhaustion, usually by about an hour after closing time, we'd sometimes have to carry him to the door and 'heave' him up onto his cart, and some nights the old horse plodded off with him lying flat on his back cackling at the stars. The old horse didn't need to be driven, he knew the way home.

There were a lot of lonely people in Betws-y-Coed, but

more than most; you had to feel sorry for Bob the Gamekeeper. Characters like Ellis Hughes had a resilience about them, but Bob needed friends and we didn't always respond.

When he asked that Friday night if I'd like to join the hunt next day I told him I was playing football.

"We'll be finished by lunch-time," he said, but I was dancing with 'Jean the Chemist' and we were too caught up in the raging atmosphere and rhythm of a 'twist' to think about foxes.

Those dance nights with the Saphires were tremendous, the beat with Len Wilcocks on the drums was out of this world, you couldn't hear yourself think, and the floor literally bounced up and down with hundreds of singing revellers rocking and twisting for hours. It was a miracle we didn't all go through to the cellars.

Roger Whittaker, who became a big star of the hit parade in the seventies, was the singer, he was a student in Bangor then, and those marvellous live band dances were so fantastic, lorry loads of Yanks used to come all the way from an air base in the Midlands, over a hundred miles away.

On that particular Friday night when Bob was recruiting for the fox hunt he was back at the bar when the dance eventually came to an end and again he collared me.

"Come and help bag a fox," he said, "we'll be finished

by lunch-time."

I told him I didn't have a gun.

"Don't worry," he said, adding with a wink, "you can use mine."

I tried to resist the offer, but his mind was made up, he was going to do somebody a favour and that night it was my turn.

"You've been in the Army," he said, "you know about guns, O.K?"

"OK" I said at last and he told me he'd arranged it all to start at nine in the morning on the Nebo Road.

The next morning the first thing I had to do was to go and pick up the gun.

I drove up to where he lived in the forest and there outside his cottage he presented me with this enormous two barrelled *Cannon.*

"It's a twin barrelled twelve bore," he said proudly, and I began to wonder how big these foxes were.

I'd been used to ordinary guns that only killed people, this thing was more like an elephant gun, but there was no turning back now and stuffing a dozen or more cartridges into my pocket I set off in my old van for the Nebo Road, Bob having explained that he was going up on foot through the forest to see the beaters.

At the bottom of the hill there was a group of men and boys carrying sticks, 'watering' the trees. 'Beaters' I said to myself, acclimatising myself to the jargon and accelerating up the road came next to a group carrying guns, a small group, just a handful of farmers, all men, no boys, 'the elite'. I was beginning to feel important. I pulled into the side, shouldered arms and joined the regiment.

No one said a word. They were all strangers to me. I exchanged a grunt or two and that was it, we just stood around waiting in silence for a couple of minutes. I was trying to think of something intelligent to ask. By the time I'd decided it was best not to ask the questions that were worrying me most like, which way up do these bullets go in? or, is it costly to kill a beater? two men came into view and there was immediate activity.

One was coming up the road, the other, Bob the gamekeeper, was approaching quietly through the trees.

'Good', I thought, 'Bob will get things moving', but it was the other who turned out to be the boss. I should have known better, I don't think Bob had anything to do with it.

The burly type who was obviously in charge, gathered us around him and issued loud and apparently detailed instructions, all in Welsh. I didn't understand a word, and all I could do was stand and watch them in turn, nod and shake their heads. It looked pretty serious and I looked around for Bob but he'd vanished.

When the man with all the say had had his say, he led us from the road and down a forest track. As the ragged little army trundled along I decided I'd better say something.

I cleared my throat. "Excuse me," I said, "where are we going?"

They stopped dead, and turning they looked at me in amazement. For a moment I thought I was going to be accused of spying.

"Who are you then?" the big man asked, and when I told him, he heaved a bit of a sigh and looked around at the others. When no one offered any comment he turned back to me and explained that we were going to form a line across a gap in the trees and wait for the beaters. He looked then at my gun.

"Do you know what you're doing with that?" he asked.

I told him I had some idea and he shrugged his shoulders.

No one else said anything to me as we moved off again, they just chatted and laughed among themselves and I was beginning to feel pretty unwelcome, but I reckoned to walk out on them now might get me shot for desertion and I took my place in the ambush.

We were looking down a wide gap in the dense pine forest, it was possibly a fire break, but you couldn't see more than about two hundred yards because of an abundant growth of bushes and saplings, but already we could hear the beaters. As we took up our positions, with each man either standing or kneeling behind a tree about twelve feet apart, we could hear them shouting down in the valley below.

I stole a glance at the gunmen either side of me. It was ridiculous, we were only ambushing a fox, but beads of sweat were beginning to show on their foreheads. I began to wonder if there was a penalty for missing.

There must have been a dozen of us strung out through those trees and apart from the sound of the distant beaters, our part of the forest was frozen in absolute silence. I tried to spot the others, but by then even the two nearest me had sunk almost out of sight.

To be honest, I didn't expect a fox to turn up. With all the military precision that had been thrown into the exercise, it seemed the very last thing that was likely to happen, but ... even as those thoughts were drifting through my mind, it also occurred to me that it was just possible that at the furthest limit of my vision ... the grass was moving.

The grass was long down there where it was exposed to the sun, and there was just the slightest suggestion that it had stirred. I watched it like a hawk, not only that stretch of grass but also a barren patch much nearer this end of it, because if there was a fox moving in that grass, he was coming forward.

Suddenly, I could see his face. It was a fox. He was peering out of the cover sizing up his next move. The barren patch was no more than a yard or two from where the long grass gave way to some bushes, and when at last he moved he was across it like a little silent streak of lightning. It was a long way off and for a while I lost sight of him altogether, but I picked him up again as he slid round a bush and then again as he stepped right out into the open to sniff the air. He decided though to press on. He was obviously concerned about the beaters by the course he was plotting, picking his way gradually up the hill away from them. His progress was slow and ponderous but clearly he would soon be within the range of our guns. The trouble was, never having fired a shotgun before, I had no idea what distance that range would be.

He stopped for another sniff, sampling the air slowly and thoughtfully. He was more suspicious now, but eventually, with the sound of the beaters getting closer and closer, he continued to come towards us.

I had him perfectly in my sights now. I was breathing deep and slow. All that National Service stuff had come back to me. I'd levelled the gun upon him so gently I'd hardly moved, but as my finger caressed the first trigger there were questions begging for answers. How much pressure could that trigger take? and why the hell hadn't anyone shot the thing already?

There was no answer to the first question and as far as the second one was concerned, the beast had to be out of range still.

It came on a few more yards, and still no one fired.

It stopped again and sampled the air, and still no one shot it. "This is ridiculous," I said to myself, "these shot guns must be useless," and when the fox disappeared between some bushes I thought we'd seen the last of it, but when it emerged even closer you could have hit it with a brick, and still no one fired at it.

"OK, OK," our leader declared as he stepped out from behind his tree, one arm aloft as a signal for us to put up our guns and break off the engagement.

I looked back to the fox. It had gone.

I engaged the safety catch and hoping they'd all done the same, joined them for the post mortem.

With the beaters now arriving on the scene they chatted away in Welsh naturally for about five minutes with everybody pointing in different directions until, like a flock of birds that has suddenly made up its mind which way to go, they all flocked off towards the road, presumably in search of another fox.

"Excuse me," I said, "why didn't we shoot this fox?"

Oliver Twist couldn't have caused a greater shock. Again they stopped dead in their tracks and stared at me.

"What fox?" the big man asked.

I looked at him and he looked at me. You could have heard the drop of a pine needle.

"That fox," I said at last, jerking my head in the direction it had come from.

His eyebrows narrowed in the way that eyebrows do when a man's working out whether you're pulling his leg or calling him a fool.

"What do you mean that fox?" he said: realising I wasn't pulling his leg.

I couldn't believe it. It was incredible, they were acting as if they hadn't seen it.

"I mean *that* fox," I said again and they all broke into dark Welsh mutterings. I looked around them all for one to back me up, but from muttering they were starting to smirk.

"It was over there," I said striding off into the undergrowth. "It was there about twenty yards away."

The laughter grew louder. I couldn't believe it, not one of them had seen it, and it was quite obvious they thought I was a lunatic.

"Why didn't *you* shoot it then?" the leader asked with a sudden grin, and with that the laughter got louder.

"Come on then," he insisted, "why didn't you shoot it if you thought you saw a fox?"

I tried to explain that I didn't know if it was in range.

That made them laugh all the more and they all turned their backs on me. Their laughter died away suddenly as the big man said something, and judging by the looks I got as we walked back to the road, he'd probably been suggesting they treat me with a measure of pity. After all what could an Englishman know about shooting foxes.

At the road there was another brief discussion and while the beaters trooped off through the trees, the 'guns' started up the hill, with me, by now a total outcast, following at the rear.

When we'd gone a little way up this steep little road, I noticed the big man whispering to another. The other man nodded to him and turning back to me as we came to a gap in the wall, our leader told me briefly his new plan.

In a nutshell, it was to leave me behind, but he actually said, "We're going to take up positions along this wall. You take the first position," and with that he pointed to this gap in the wall, ushered me through it and hurried on to catch up with the others, shouting back to me, "we'll spread out round the corner."

They did too. They carried on up the road, round the bend, out of sight and out of earshot too eventually as the sound of their boots faded away on the crisp still air.

Not knowing what to do, I slumped down with my back against the wall and peered gloomily through the trees. There was no open run up between them here, it was just

53

a thick black forest, and there was no sound of beaters in the distance either, they weren't in this part that was for sure. I'd been dumped.

As I sat there cradling the gun across my lap I felt so depressed I even started to doubt my own sanity.

'Had I seen a fox? Could I have seen a fox?'

"Dammit," I said aloud, "of course I saw a fox. I watched it for at least ten minutes."

The Nebo Road is a very quiet road, very few cars use it, but if someone had been walking up there while I was talking to myself that would have been the end. I would certainly have been branded a lunatic then.

I was sorely tempted to go and leave them all to it, but as I laid back my mind turned to other things.

A couple of buzzards were wheeling and dealing so high up in the sky they looked no bigger than a couple of specks, but the air was so calm their high pitched calls were clear and unmistakable. I watched them for a few minutes and gradually my thoughts turned to football.

I can't remember all these years later who we were playing that Saturday, but I'd just got into the local team at Betws-y-Coed and I badly needed a goal that afternoon. If I was going to live in the Conway Valley I dare not have another failure like I'd had that morning. A dozen farmers now thought I was crazy, but if I could knock in a few goals I might yet survive.

I was just wondering how many I needed to score when I heard something.

Whatever it was it was very faint, it had been nothing more than the slightest suggestion of *something,* something deep down among those trees.

For a long time I sat peering down the slope beneath the dense green branches of the fir trees, peering into the empty blackness. For a long time I watched and waited, the gun now following my gaze.

I knew I'd heard something, and eventually, oh so eventually, he came into view. He was just a shadow within shadows at first, but gradually as he came towards the light he grew bigger and bigger. He was coming straight up the hill towards me. It was a fox, and he was *enormous.*

He was approaching so very cautiously, and I was watching him so intensely that the only sound in the world I could hear now was the beating of my heart. I knew that I had to shoot that fox, and I had to do it on my own.

He was big, really big, but in spite of his size, he made no sound on the carpet of brown pine needles.

When he was no more than twenty yards away, I pulled the trigger.

As the explosion ripped through my ears and the butt of the gun kicked back into my shoulder, he screamed, he literally screamed as he was thrown back against a tree, and then, he slumped to the ground dead.

I skated down under the branches and knelt over him, and I felt so sorry for him. It's strange but the feeling took me by surprise, and I was glad my shot had got him right through the head and he wasn't now tearing off to die hours or even days later.

I did feel sorry for him, he was a beautiful animal, but then I looked at his teeth, and I thought of all the lambs and chickens he would have slaughtered, and as I pulled him up to the road I could hear the sound of heavy boots running like mad down the hill. I could hear them shouting too. It was pretty obvious they thought I'd shot myself.

When they saw the fox they went wild. I was mobbed. It was very embarrassing. They slapped my back until it was sore, and the big man shook my hand until my arm nearly came out of its socket.

They turned out to be a really nice bunch. They wanted to know where I'd learnt to shoot and, of course, they all wanted to know about the other fox down the road, amazed now that they hadn't seen it, and their leader shaking his head and looking so apologetic started shaking my hand all over again.

As the tight circle around me started to thin out however, I spotted another movement beneath the trees. Bob the Gamekeeper was coming up the same way as the fox had come.

He stopped in the shadows, and making sure no one saw him, he gave me a thumbs up sign, and then with a nod he turned and melted away, back down into the shadows of the forest.

oooooOooooo

It will always be a mystery of course, but I've often wondered if that fox came with the compliments of Bob the Gamekeeper. Could he have known it was there? Could he have out-manoeuvred the beaters and driven it up to where I was sitting?

I asked him of course, several times, and I got many a bleary eyed wink and an occasional wagging finger, but never an answer.

CHAPTER 5

Like those that followed him, the first guard dog we had at the Waterloo was far removed from the 'wolves' employed by many of today's publicans and the army of security firms, but nevertheless we soon realised the need for a good 'vicious' dog and a local farmer near Trefriw sold us the perfect specimen. At least, according to the farmer he was the perfect specimen, but I had my doubts about him right from the start.

It was just after the last of the great oak trees had been felled that he arrived with my father following on the end of a bit of string. As guard dogs go he was a sort of fly weight, mostly black as I recall, but for the life of me I can't remember his name, he was such an insignificant little thing. I doubt if he weighed more than a ginger tom, but at least this pip squeak of a dog had a voice to his credit. It wasn't so much of a bark, more of a yelp however and it went on day and night, and for the first couple of nights, instead of guarding the hotel, he had to be shut away in one of the stables in a hopeless effort to stop him from keeping people awake.

The other problem with him was that he kept running off.

The farmer wasn't worried. "Just keep him chained

up," he said.

My father on the other hand had a better idea. "We'll build him a kennel round the back in a strategic position," he said, "where he can see all the comings and goings around the back of the hotel and we'll make it big enough for him to walk around inside so he doesn't have to be chained up. You mark my words," he said, "that's where we need him. If someone tries to break in they'll come that way, down through the woods, along the railway, down the back drive, and at the slightest movement he'll bark."

That all seemed to make sense, and it was decided the best place for him would be in the 'lean-to' shed. This was alongside a row of derelict stables and it could also be reached through a door from the car park.

"You can't keep him in a kennel for ever," my Auntie Joyce said.

"Don't worry it's just a matter of *training*," my father assured her, sounding now like a circus owner. "When he's used to being there we can start leaving the door open and he can come and go as he pleases."

So it was then that work started on providing this tiny dog with an enormous kennel by partitioning off a whole section of the shed using floorboards borrowed from the top floor of the hotel.

It was one of those bright sunny mornings when

anything in the world seemed possible. My father and Bob got to work in the shed, and between serving the occasional gallon of petrol, I started to clear away the remaining branches from the last oak tree we'd felled on the car park.

We had in fact intended to keep that one, and consequently the tarmac had been laid around it, but in the end my father reckoned it was obscuring the place from view and so like the others, we brought it crashing to the ground.

However, I'd been looking forward to this particular day. Now that the petrol station was becoming established and running well, I'd decided to populate it with female attendants in leopard skin trousers. This I felt would sustain my interest and bring in extra customers, and that afternoon I had a girl coming for an interview. The first one. I was looking forward to that because I'd have to measure her legs.

Unfortunately, the day began to deteriorate. My father's joinery was to blame. A few days earlier he'd erected a large sign on the far side of the road declaring that this was the Waterloo and Bed and Breakfast was 17/6, and he'd put it up on a couple of posts. It was high enough to walk under, but the six inch nails he'd used had split the old worm-eaten posts from top to bottom. Consequently, just as I was about to tackle the oak tree branches, there was a loud crash and the sign was found to be lying in the road. Cars and lorries were swerving around it as if they were on a racetrack rounding a chicane.

There followed an exchange of words between my father and I as to whose fault it was and who should put it up again. It finished with him saying he was too busy and I'd have to put it up, but with the petrol station air pump now going wrong and a delivery of oil gone astray, it wasn't the best time to be patching up his joinery, especially as he had the hammer.

I think the basic difference between father and son on these occasions was that he believed in mending split wood with more nails today, and I believed in mending split wood with more wood tomorrow. So for the time being I pushed the sign back up into what looked like a fairly upright position, and propped it up with a scaffolding plank.

The day got worse, in fact it grew worse with every passing hour. The air pump that had been playing up, packed up altogether, and the girl didn't turn up to have her legs measured.

Bob and my father however did manage to finish the Dog House. It was so big you certainly couldn't call it a kennel. According to my father one end was all wire netting so the dog could keep a watch on the back drive, and it had a wire netting door so he could look the other way too.

I wasn't too sure he was going to take the job all that seriously, but he was taken, bouncing on the end of a rope for a slap-up meal in the snack bar and then after a run round the car park, he was put into his new home for the night.

Next morning he was gone.

We stood deep in thought. In silence we just stood there, Bob, my father and I, we just stood there. My father lighting his pipe, and Bob with a hand under his cap scratching his head.

The door was still closed and fastened, but he wasn't there. You could *see* he wasn't there. It was a proper mystery. A Sherlock Holmes or a Sexton Blake, or rather – a Father Brown – with the chill of the night still on the morning air and the raucous call of a lone crow somewhere in the distance. It had that sort of rural earthy feeling to it.

It was Bob who broke the silence. "Well, I don't know boss," he said, and then said it a few more times.

"I bet you he's been stolen," I said, and my father, shaking out his match and throwing it over his shoulder with accustomed irritability, asked why anyone would want to steal a dog?

"To make it safer to break in," I said, but he said that was nonsense, and engulfing us in blue smoke, asked why, if that was the case, had they taken the trouble to close and fasten the door.

Bob wondered if it was to confuse us.

Bending down, my father showed us he'd already worked out how the dog had got out. "There you are," he said, "He's pushed the door out at the bottom, it needs fastening at the bottom as well."

It was quite disappointing really, and it wasn't all that much of a relief when later that morning, the little brute turned up.

When I say 'turned up' I don't mean he came home fully repentant with his tail between his legs, far from it. I'd repaired the air pump and I was again struggling to clear the branches from the car park, when I spotted him cheerfully trotting up the road from the village. By the way he was licking his lips, he'd been down someone's bin. As soon as he saw me though, he stopped, and then of course he quickly jumped over the wall and shot off through the orchard to the river. There was no one wanting petrol, so I leapt over the wall and gave chase.

At that moment Bob came looking for the plank.

My father's philosophy had been 'either the dog comes back or we get another one' and he'd therefore commandeered Bob to help him mend and strengthen the dog house from top to bottom.

Joyce was up to her armpits doing more washing, my

mother was preparing to start cooking lunches and Sid was complaining that he needed change for the tills, but my father had more important things to do. The dog house had to be made dog proof.

While he banged more nails into *everything*, he sent Bob for something to strengthen the doorframe. The best thing to use, they both agreed, was the scaffolding plank I kept hidden behind the petrol station.

Bob of course couldn't find it there, but eventually he spotted it leaning against the sign at the side of the road, only of course it wasn't leaning against it, it was holding it up.

Now, on any other day it wouldn't have mattered but that morning was rather special, and indeed that particular hour was crucial.

Earlier there had been some mention of the event, but I personally had forgotten all about it. I heard the loudspeaker car as it came over the Waterloo Bridge, but I was too busy trying to catch the dog to pay much attention, and it wasn't until I had at last cornered the thing, dived on it and scooped it up, that I realised the race was coming through.

It was a cycle race, and as I crossed the road ahead of them, a policeman on a motorbike warned me to keep hold of the dog, but my eyes were firmly rooted on Bob. Totally oblivious to the race coming up behind him, he was removing the all-important plank.

I shouted to him to leave it there, but my voice was drowned by the motorbike and shouts of encouragement to the riders from people parked in the kerb.

As he walked off down the road with it on his shoulder, the sign wavered for a moment and then slowly started to topple forward. Someone shouted 'look out' and two men leapt from a car and grabbed hold of it, managing to hold it up as the cyclists hurtled past, and Bob, still with the plank over his shoulder, turned to see what had happened.

Up until that moment very little had happened, but when Bob and the plank swung round the on-coming cyclists let out an almighty yell and were sent careering all over the road, crashing into each other, pushing and shoving, shouting and swearing, and all Bob could do was stand there in amazement, asking where they'd come from.

Fortunately, they didn't stop to tell him in any great detail and were on their way again even as I grabbed hold of the plank and threw him the dog.

"Go and chain this thing up somewhere quick," I said, and as he wandered off completely bewildered I propped the sign up with the plank again.

By the time my father arrived on the scene a couple of race officials were there to lodge a complaint.

"The riders will be coming back through here again later on the return leg," they said, "we'll be reporting this sign to the Police," and with that they drove off.

My father asked me again to fix it. The request coming in no uncertain terms, but with the traffic moving once more I was busy serving petrol and when Bob wobbled off on his bike for lunch and my father went off to Llanrwst for more nails, the sign still hadn't been touched.

Lunch for me was usually something on my lap in the kiosk, but that day I went without while I rooted around between serving customers for some wood. I didn't do very well. There was nothing really long enough and it was nearly all too rotten to nail together.

I gave up when I heard the familiar clatter of buckets on the wall. The head of the local constabulary, the police sergeant, had arrived in the field alongside to feed his sheep.

As he tipped the buckets into their trough, he was visibly deep in thought. "That incident this morning," he said with a sigh, "it might have been very awkward you know."

I had to agree.

"They could probably sue you know," he said.

I suggested Bob could plead insanity.

"Well no it's the sign you see," he said, beginning to sound depressingly like my father.

He climbed over the gate and dumping his buckets by the pumps dawdled across to inspect it.

"I think you'd better keep that plank against it," he said on returning. "It could fall down otherwise you know."

I agreed and we then discussed the things we normally discussed, the weather, the state of the river, and foot rot.

We talked until Bob freewheeled onto the forecourt shouting greetings to the sergeant and slithering off in his normal fashion against the diesel pump.

The sergeant picked up his buckets and as he strolled off, Bob and I got down to clearing away the last of that pile of branches.

Except for the jukebox in the snack bar blasting the Shadows 'Apache' out of an open window it was very quiet. There was very little traffic passing now and there was absolutely nothing on the car park.

When at last one car did pull in, it swept round to the snack bar just as we were dragging away the last branch, but it didn't stop. It slowed down but continued to do circles and figures of eight all over the place.

We stood spellbound by this strange behaviour. The car was being driven by an old man who was very small and was having great difficulty in seeing over the steering wheel. He seemed to be totally confused by the ocean of empty tarmac. An elderly woman was sitting next to him and it might have been his wife, but between them they didn't seem to be able to make up their minds where to park.

The car park was completely empty except for one thing of course, the big tree stump. The old chap must have seen it there, he must have done, but before long he was on it. He drove straight up onto it and there he was, high and dry with one wheel spinning off the ground.

That really pleased Bob. "You're off the ground," he shouted, and they wound down the windows and peered out. It must have been excruciatingly embarrassing and Bob was making the most of it.

"You're on the tree. Didn't you see it?" He was laughing so much he could hardly stand up. "We'll make it bigger for you next time," he was saying.

A couple of hitchhikers and the girls from the snack bar came out to see what was going on and gathered round the car with the old couple sitting there in stony silence. They were like a couple of stranded passengers on a broken down fairground ride.

I tried rocking the car to slide it off either backwards or forwards, but it was stuck fast. All I was doing was bouncing the occupants up and down. Not that they objected, they just sat there staring into space.

"What we need is a lever Bob," I said, "a long bit of timber perhaps."

As soon as the words were out I hastily tried to retrieve them in case he went for the plank. I didn't want him telling my father I still hadn't mended the sign.

"Anything will do," I said quickly. "It doesn't have to be wood, a long bit of metal will do."

"How about a railway line?" he suggested.

"Yes, good thinking Bob," I said, impressed by this instant response.

"We haven't got a railway line Nox."

"Well something *like* a railway line," I said.

"Something *like* a railway line," he murmured thoughtfully.

It was beginning to sound like a T.V. panel game. The onlookers were giving us strange looks.

"Something like a railway line," he said again, rubbing his grey stubbled chin. "Difficult one this, Nox."

I was also racking my brains hard. "I've got it," I said quickly, "a branch! A branch will do," and I went over to where we'd dumped the last of the oak tree branches and dragged back one of the longest.

I roped in the hitchhikers to help and between us we managed to tip the car up enough for it to drive off backwards.

The driver was visibly relieved, and after a discussion with his passenger he eventually got out and produced from the boot, a bottle of wine.

"Only home made plonk," he said meekly "I made it myself."

Bob held out his hand for it but I beat him to it. I thanked the man and he thanked me. He thanked Bob and Bob thanked him. I thanked Bob and Bob thanked me. It was very civilised but it was getting out of hand, the old girl was getting out the car now. She thanked me. I thanked her, she thanked Bob, Bob bowed and again the old boy thanked me and again I said "It was a pleasure," and so it went on.

They eventually left without visiting the snack bar or anywhere else come to that, the dining room, the bar, or even the toilets.

"What shall we do with the wine Nox?"

I knew that question was coming. "I'll keep it in the kiosk," I answered, already on my way to the petrol station as my father arrived back. He'd hardly got out of the car before Bob was telling him of the events of the last half hour, reliving with relish every exaggerated detail, including the fact that we'd been given a bottle of wine.

As I sat waiting for customers I could soon hear the hammering up in the dog house getting louder and louder. It was a sure sign that my father was running out of patience. Every now and then the dog would start yelping. It sounded as if it was being nailed down!

When at long last the lad from the village arrived after school for the teatime shift on the petrol pumps, I was itching to see what had been going on up there.

One of my assistants eventually went to the House of Commons as the local Member of Parliament for Plaid Cymru, but whether it was Elfyn that day I can't remember, but as soon as I could, I left the pumps and went to see how the builders were getting on.

The timing was perfect unfortunately. As I went up the steps and opened the door into the stables, they were just finishing. The whole thing was now bigger and stronger, strengthened with many more borrowed floorboards. It would have held a tiger. It would have stood up to an avalanche. It had wire mesh visibility on three sides now instead of just two, and yet it was so much sturdier. There was no way that dog was going to squeeze out of there.

He never did either.

"Right," my father declared, "we'll put him in. Bob, get the dog."

"Yes sir," Bob said with enthusiasm, attempting to unchain him.

He wasn't very good with dogs though. The beast was all over him straight away, and my father, who was no better, tried to take over.

As they struggled with it I thought I heard a loudspeaker. I opened the door and looked out across the car park just in time to see the loudspeaker van going back along the main road. Just as it had been doing that morning, it was blasting out a crackly message about the cycle race.

"The leaders are coming through now," the voice was saying. "Please keep to one side."

Suddenly there were frantic shouts behind me. My father was yelling to me to shut the door but it was too late, the dog shot between my legs, flew down the steps and accelerated across the car park like a greyhound.

As we gathered in the doorway, the cyclists came into view. One moment they were peddling away in a compact orderly group, the next they were all over the place with our dog zigzagging through the lot of them. It was chaos. One hit a tree, another went over the wall.

We closed the door and stood there for a few moments, saying nothing.

We never saw that dog again. He completely disappeared.

We returned to the hotel via the back way, and waited in the front bar for the Police to arrive. Sid and my mother thought it was funny enough but Joyce was having hysterics. My father was far from happy of course and was raking his pipe out in the fireplace, but after about half an hour no one had come knocking on the door and we reckoned the dog must have been considered to be a stray.

Things were looking a lot brighter. Bob was sent to the snack bar to ask Mrs Jones to make a fresh pot of tea, but Joyce had a better idea.

"Where's that bottle of wine that old chap gave you?"

"It's out at the petrol station," I said, "Shall we try it?"

"Good idea," my father agreed, deciding to brighten up. "Bob!" he shouted through the hatch to the snack bar. "Don't bother with the tea."

Bob appeared looking confused.

My aunt tried to get through to him.

"Bob," she shouted, "get the plonk."

Bob hesitated and still looked puzzled. Then raising a finger to signify that the penny had dropped, he turned and was gone.

While we waited, my father and I were looking out the window, just vacantly staring into space really. Every now and then a car passed. Then Bob passed. He was trudging along with the plank on his shoulder.

In silence my father looked at me and I looked at him. Quickly then we peered down the road. The sign was slowly bending forward.

A lorry was approaching. The driver braked, the sign fell, the driver changed his mind, and ran over it.

CHAPTER 6

When we went to the Waterloo I swear we were all sane, but there was *something,* something in the atmosphere of that place which was capable of dissolving sanity. We used to wonder if it was something in the water, but it might have been something in the air, a form of Radon gas, or perhaps it was the dry-rot, but whatever it was, it was highly contagious. I fell for a pig.

oooooOooooo

Sally was my sow and she was my pride and joy. As soon as I saw her standing serenely with the green mud bubbling up around her ankles in that Dolwyddelan field, I knew I had to have her. Even if I had to sell my car to pay for her I knew I had to make her my own.

Haggling over the price was a long and arduous affair and now all these years later I can't recall how much I paid for her. I think the cost was erased from my mind almost immediately. Fixing a price for a creature of such beauty was too sordid a business to file into memory.

On the other hand, it couldn't have been too much because I kept my car. It was a black Ford Popular and I bought it from George Oldham for £5. He was a nice chap but he knew how to drive a hard bargain.

What I remember about that car was the cylinder head gasket going almost immediately, but then I also recall its remarkable windscreen wiper. It was powered by air pressure. The harder it rained or snowed the faster you had to drive to see where you were going, but when he sold it to me, I remember him sitting on his favourite stool in the front bar explaining they were becoming very rare cars, and he was right of course. Mine was extinct within six months.

For transporting a sow however, I had to use the hotel's 'bus', the old van I carried waitresses and cleaners in, seated in those days before seat belts, on stools and deck chairs, and arriving home with the world's biggest pig was a proud moment. Several of my friends were there to greet us and my mother was pleased. She would have preferred a steady girlfriend but Sally was undeniably a superb bit of stuff. She was about seven foot long, she must have weighed half a ton and she could probably have bitten your leg off, but she was a beauty. As far as I was concerned nothing was too good for her. I fed her on the best dinners the hotel could produce.

I'd had quite a few pigs before, little weaners that I bought from an old friend called Peter the Pig, to fatten up to pork weight in one of the stables, but Sally was going to change all that. She was going to present me with weaners for free.

When I bought her from this farmer up in the Lledr Valley, he assured me she was "fully serviced" as he put it, but I really should have got it in writing.

Thinking I'd got myself a pregnant pig, I put her in the stable to await the great day and decided without hesitation that having a proper big pig was far superior to having a stable full of little pigs. Nothing on the face of this earth can drive you mad faster than a dozen piglets. When they're not eating, they're chewing the handle off the door, or pushing out the window frame, and running off with your tools when you come to mend it. When you've got your hammer back another's got the screwdriver. You get the screwdriver back and the pinchers have been pinched. And if you think piglets squeal at you, they don't. They giggle at you.

However, I suppose nothing matures quite like a pig. Nothing slows down quite so rapidly from the pink lightening of youth to stolid maturity within such a short period of time, and a sow becomes such a dependable creature of habit, her delivery date can be marked on the calendar as soon as she's mated. Three months, three weeks, and three days – if I remember correctly.

Unfortunately, the man I bought my sow from said he couldn't remember the day she was mated, and so for weeks I fed her and I gave her fresh straw to lie on every day and put her feet up when she looked tired, but there was no sign of morning sickness and she didn't develop any special craving, she just ate everything in sight.

Eventually I gave up waiting for her to deliver. Old Bob said he saw a stork sitting by the railway one morning but when I looked it was only a heron, and it was obvious I had to have her done again, so I took her in the van to George Jones' boar in Llanrwst.

I don't know if it was love at first sight but it was pretty potent whatever it was.

With tremendous dignity she walked down the sagging plank and as the springs of the van heaved a sigh of relief, she strolled through the gate into the arena.

The boar, I forget his name, was three fields away but straight away he caught a whiff of her perfume, and with hardly a moment's pause for thought he plodded slowly towards her.

George said "he'll do you," which I took to mean 'he'll do OK', but stepped back a bit just in case, and watched in silent admiration as he casually ploughed through the barbarous hedges of blackthorn as if they were honeysuckle.

Slowly he lumbered on and even before he reached her she obligingly turned and presented her rear end to him, and when at last he arrived at that moment of impact, he heaved himself up onto her with an almighty grunt. It was like watching two laborious old goods trains collide. Slowly he piled up on top of her, steam and sinews wheezing and creaking as the whole heap threatened to collapse.

When at last it was over George said, "In the end you have to do it yourself" which I took to mean something altogether different, and discreetly we withdrew to let them introduce themselves, and perhaps indulge in another collision for luck.

As the weeks of her pregnancy went by, I decided to find her somewhere better to live, and after careful thought decided to build her an ark so that she could enjoy a run in the open air.

This 'Ark' structure, popular at the time with pig farmers everywhere, resembled an upside down V and the advantages were two-fold, three even. In the first place it could accommodate her somewhere where she could get some sunshine, and secondly the sloping sides of the ark would give protection to the newly borne piglets, making it virtually impossible for them to be squashed by their mother. The other reason wasn't so important, not nearly as important, but it would do some of my mates a favour.

Over the course of a year or so, I'd let a crowd of fellow walkers/climbers, bed down at weekends in the hayloft over her stable, and with the holes in the hayloft floor allowing free passage of warm rising air, it was extremely smelly. Not that it stopped them coming. As a form of central heating it was unique. In fact if they'd used their heads they might have cooked on it. It was probably pure methane.

The mate who'd originally asked me about somewhere to turn into a bunk-house was a lad called Bill, and to begin with it was just for him and a couple of his mates, but gradually the number grew. Most of them were from Merseyside and not much younger than myself. Mostly they sat on walls in the sun and in cafes in the wet, looking for girls. Some of course brought their own and the only climbing they did was over each other.

My father wouldn't have approved, but with hundreds of scruffs sleeping rough in barns and tents all over the place he couldn't tell who was sleeping where, or come to that, who was male and who was female at that time of visual unisex.

It was never actually a den of vice, it was a hideout, an escape for those still young enough to escape. A hide out alongside the railway in a loft behind all the other ruins, and soon they'd found an old stove for it and in no time a bit of cast iron drainpipe had sprouted through the slates to act as a chimney. It was damp but cosy, the air thick with the smell of baked beans, wet socks and Sally, who sat grunting below waiting for the plates to be scraped through the holes in the floor.

However, things hadn't been going too well for Bill. His generosity had thrown the place open to too many bodies. I spent many an evening up there and it just got more and more crowded and now that he'd met a girl he'd really fallen for, he had nowhere to be alone with her.

She was very nice, far too nice to bed down with that crowd in the loft, and when she turned up to meet him in the bar on a Saturday night, he'd hide away with her in a corner where they'd sit quietly together all the evening until melting away into the night by closing time.

I don't know where she came from, on the Wirral somewhere I think, but she used to come with another couple of girls who had a caravan somewhere in Betws, and after he'd taken her back there, Bill would return to the stable loft looking a proper misery. The new age of sexual freedom in the Sixties was nothing like as easy as it was supposed to be, and for a while Bill disappeared altogether. It was clear that the course of true love was on the rocks.

I caught sight of her on a couple of occasions sitting demurely with her girlfriends, saying nothing as usual, but for about a month there was no sign of young Bill.

"He's trying to forget her," one of his mates shouted above the din one night as I collected his glass. "He thinks she's too good for him."

"What does she think?" I asked and he shrugged his

shoulders.

"Don't know till you try," he said and pushing through the crowd he went over and tried to chat her up.

Next time I looked, the girls had gone and he was sitting there alone.

The following weekend Bill was back. He and she were sitting together as usual and he was looking as glum as ever, but life had to go on, I had a home to build for my Sally and I was ready to build the ark.

There was one drawback however. The next morning my father vetoed my plans to build it with floor boards, but the marvellous thing about the old Waterloo was its sheer size and spread, and literally crawling under a forest of Rhododendrons I explored a part of the ruined stables I'd not fully examined before and miraculously it opened up a whole new set of potentials.

There were floor boards in good condition in the end building, and a little extension on the car park side was so dry it dawned on me that it would make another bunkhouse, in fact a proper bunkhouse that we could charge a nightly fee for, and for the next hour I was scrambling into the rest of the hovels alongside, devoured by a fresh passion to convert the whole row into a block of self-contained climbing huts, a sort of up market dossers motel, lit with oil lamps and equipped with primus stove-cookers and done out with old climbing ropes and crampons and pictures of Hillery and Tensing on Everest.

I was so convinced I was onto a winner I left the useable floorboards in place, but of course I knew the main problem would be winning over my father. He'd recently thrown a dozen of my climbing mates out of the front bar for drying their underpants on a poker, and sooner or later he was going to find them sleeping up by the railway, but I felt sure that once he saw the money making potential he'd not only come round to my way of thinking, but before long he'd be claiming it was his idea.

The following week I had to go to Jones & Bebb and buy expensive new wood to build the ark. It was a bit painful but at least it showed how much I thought of my Sally, and the corrugated iron for the roof was even more expensive.

By the end of the week, after I'd devoted every hour of my spare time to it, the ark was finished and it was a masterpiece. I even hung a sackcloth curtain at the entrance to keep the rain out.

The location for my blossoming pig farm was in the jungle beyond the Coach House, and I assembled the ark in the remains of an old Nisson Hut, possibly built during the war. The curved corrugated roof had long since collapsed and rusted away, or more likely had been stolen, and I was left with a long concrete area surrounded by four brick walls three foot high, and furthermore, hidden away in that jungle were five more identical pens.

As soon as I got away from the petrol station, once the Saturday morning lad arrived, I took Sally up to her new home. As it turned out it was only to be a fleeting visit.

For some one born a town boy like me, having a pig of that size requires all the skill of a lion tamer. Holding a broom in one hand and a dustbin lid in the other, you hover round its back-end half demanding, half persuading it to go in the right direction until with luck, you arrive at the right place, and it was somewhere in the middle of this navigation that I heard a distant crash.

It was the sort of noise regularly caused by my father and Bob so I took no great notice and when we reached the ark Sally took one sniff at it and pushed straight in. With a few grunts she managed to turn round a couple of times, causing the corrugated roof to swell and bulge, and with a look of approval on her face she lumbered out to explore the yard. It was then that I made a serious mistake.

There's no room for manoeuvre in a sow's ark, the whole point of it is that it's only just big enough for the thing to lie down with its piglets without trampling on them, and when I crawled in to check it over, it suddenly went very dark. The only sound in the whole world was the sound of heavy breathing and it wasn't mine. I knew without turning round I was trapped.

When I did turn round it was very slowly. She was

completely filling the entrance, the bit of sack perched on the top of her head like a silly hat, and as I knelt there staring into her little beady blue eyes, her grunts turned to a throaty growl. I was by now feeling far from happy. I couldn't back away and I couldn't stand up. I was totally at the mercy of that enormous mouthful of brown molars and whatever was ticking over in that mysterious mind.

Large pigs can occasionally be very vicious, but all I could do was say nice things to it. Things like, "Who's a nice little piggy then?" and all the time those little blue eyes stared back at me with icy inscrutability, and as the cold sweat trickled down my back I felt like a sacrificial goat.

I remember being quite relieved when at last she decided to withdraw, but withdraw she eventually did, and I followed her like a shot and took her straight back to the stable. I had to fix up a heater lamp inside the ark before she gave birth and there was no way I was going to do that with her around.

Altogether it was a most disappointing end to the morning, and when I got down to the car park there was another disappointment waiting for me.

I noticed the bus standing in the road and wondered what it was doing there. It was a normal green single decker Crosville bus and the passengers were just sitting there doing nothing. Some I recognised. There were a couple of our cleaners, presumably looking for a better job, and 'Scoop Thomas' the local reporter, presumably chasing after a news story. He always went by bus. They all looked very bored and goodness knows how long they'd been waiting because the driver, instead of sitting behind the wheel, was over by the stables.

It was another local pig breeder. This one was *Gwilym* the pig, and on this occasion even more jovial than usual; standing laughing with old Bob in the midst of a pile of bricks.

Bob had a crow bar in his hands, and the bricks were all that was left of my new bunkhouse.

"He wants 'em for a new pig sty Nox," Bob shouted, and Gwilym the pig waved a brick.

That night after my evening stint on the petrol pumps I came in and I suppose I had a few pints too many. I sat in the bar reflecting on the meaning of life, totally oblivious to everything going on around me. It really had been a rotten day. I couldn't believe my pig could have looked at me like that.

At first there was nothing out of the ordinary about the kit bag lying on the floor by the dart board. Kit bags and rucksacks just littered the place at weekends, but after a while I began to realise this kit bag was different to all the other kit bags. This long sausage shaped khaki lump was occasionally 'twitching'. For long periods it lay hidden from view by dozens of legs, but every now and then the human tide parted, and every now and then it twitched.

I began to realise that no ordinary kit bag should ever lie on the floor twitching. The one I'd had in the army had never twitched.

Once I'd woken up to the fact that I wasn't seeing things, I hauled myself up from the armchair to investigate, but the crowds had closed the gap again and before I could push through someone was shouting from behind the bar that there was a girl in it.

I think it was Dai or it might have been one of the lads from the forestry school, but someone had certainly shouted "there's a girl in that kit bag." And in the confusion I saw it being suddenly slung onto a shoulder and someone dashed with it out the side door. By the time I got through the crowd, most of whom were turning round asking which girl was in what, the bloke and the kit bag had disappeared into the night. Some of us ran round to the road but by then there was no sign of either him, the kit bag, or the girl.

Back in the bar a couple of blokes were saying they'd seen her face peering up from the floor but no-one gave it a second thought. The beer went on flowing, and the piano went on playing just like the Wild West, and the singing too, never stopped for a moment.

Closing time had been ages ago and soon I was getting

impatient signals from the bar to collect glasses and stumbling around on my errands I came across Bill and his girlfriend where apparently they'd been hiding in a corner all the evening, sitting there holding hands in silence as usual.

As the Welsh National Anthem was being slaughtered for about the eighth time, one of Bill's mates attempted to communicate by funnelling his hands over my ear.

"We've been trying to get Bill and his girlfriend up to the hayloft tonight," he hollered, "but she won't come."

Juggling as I was at the time over a sea of heads with a tray of glasses, it wasn't easy to catch all he was trying to say, but I gathered she was going away.

"I reckon it's tonight or never," he shouted. "You know what I mean?"

I nodded, but by then the crowds were pulling us in opposite directions and that was all I heard.

About half an hour later at last the place was empty and kicking out the dogs to do whatever dogs do before they curl up for the night, I spotted two huddled figures in the shadows beyond the petrol pumps.

Once the dogs were back in I took another look and they were still there, so I ventured across the car park.

It was of course Bill and his girlfriend, but as I approached she broke away and slowly wandered of towards the road.

"Christ, Allan" he whispered, "I can't take her in with the others. You haven't got somewhere else have you?"

I knew how he felt but there was nothing I could say. He turned and leant against a petrol pump, staring down at his boots, and I watched her waking away, slowly making for a couple of girls waiting for her up the road.

"You know," he murmured without looking up, "somewhere we could just be together."

I don't know how it occurred to me, but as I watched her walking away something started to dawn on me.

"Go and bring her back," I said, "just go and get her," and without saying any more I dashed off to get a torch and a bottle of wine.

From up in my bedroom I got a torch and a sleeping bag which I rammed into a rucksack with the bottle and a corkscrew, and slipping out the back way I met them at the top end of the car park.

I don't know why I was doing it, but at the time it seemed a good idea.

There was no moon that night, but the stars shone like diamonds as I led them in silence up the jungle path until I stopped and shone the torch on the ark.

"There you are," I said, "its brand new and never been slept in."

Without even the slightest hesitation he gave me a wink and she, silent as ever stood tightly gripping his arm as I pulled back the bit of sacking and spread the sleeping bag out over the fresh golden straw and threw in the bottle of wine.

"Thanks mate," he whispered as I handed him the torch, and as he took it a ray of light lit up her face. I think I did the right thing.

ooooo**O**ooooo

That following morning I didn't let on to the others where they'd gone. No one would have guessed they were in the ark, but in any case I think they were probably away before anyone was up.

I never saw Bill and his girlfriend again. According to his mates in the weeks that followed, they were soon engaged and he wasn't allowed out at weekends, not to Wales anyway. Rumour had it that her family had found better things for him to do.

On the Monday afternoon when business was quieter, I hung a cardboard label six foot long with 'Diesel' written on it round the diesel pump and promoted Bob to petrol pump attendant, while I went to sort out some electric cable for the ark. As I left him on the pump island, saluting like a newly commissioned captain of a corvette, I said a little prayer. He put his glasses on then, and read the label.

By teatime I'd found enough cable to go up to the ark

from the breakfast kitchen. In all I'd found fourteen lengths, some of it lead covered from the top floors where we'd ripped up the floorboards, and by taping it Waterloo fashion all into one length it went all the way, slung and strung through the trees and bushes right up to the piglet factory.

Before long I'd bought the electric heater lamp and had safely installed both lamp and pig. Strictly in that order.

As the date got closer I took every opportunity to consult the experts. Any of the local farmers, or bus drivers come to that, who knew one end of a pig from the other, were closely questioned on the complications of advanced pregnancy.

"Do you reckon I ought to be with her?" I asked Ellis Hughes, and that was a mistake for a start. He'd farmed dinosaurs in his early days and he'd lost patience with anything finicky.

"Diawl!" he spluttered in a shower of amazement. "*Be* with her? *Be* with her?" he repeated choking with scorn. "I wouldn't waste my time being with a *woman*."

Drying my face with a handkerchief as he laughed himself into a fit, I tried to explain that it might be her first time, but it was no good, he was choking so much I nearly bought him a drink.

"She'll do better without you hanging around her," he wheezed, the old dog end still miraculously hanging onto his bottom lip, even though he was now in a state of collapse.

Everyone said the same thing. "Leave her to it."

"Do you want to get in the ark with her again?" Gwilym the pig asked when he came for another load of bricks.

I shook my head.

"Leave her to it," he said beaming confidently, "she'll deliver them in the night for you, you see."

So a couple of nights before "D" day night, I switched on the lamp for her to get used to it and pitched in a mountain of fresh bedding.

It was daft but standing outside I couldn't help thinking as she settled down in there with chinks of warm yellowy light shining through the sacking, that it was a bit like a scene from the Nativity.

I had no way of knowing, but as it happened there was certainly a miracle on the way.

The next morning I took a bucket of swill up to her. It was pouring with rain but it didn't matter. That coming night was to be 'the' night, the calendar said so. At long last I was going to be a dad to a family of piglets, perhaps a dozen if I was lucky.

"Come on" I called as I approached the gate, "come on, this time tomorrow you'll be a mum."

There were no eager snorts to greet me that morning.

It was all quiet and I knew there was something wrong even before I looked over the wall.

I couldn't believe what I saw. It just broke my heart. Lying in a puddle were little rain spattered pink bodies.

The so-called mother was still in the ark.

I put down the bucket and walked slowly across the concrete and stood looking down at them. There were eleven of them, all dead. She'd had them a night early and had kicked the lot out in the rain to die.

I admit before they were born I might have seen them in my mind's eye as little bundles of fivers, but now they were real little piglets, little new born corpses, cold and wet. They looked so pitiful lying in that puddle.

I pulled back the sack and looking up at me she snorted contemptuously. I swore at her and eventually managed to pull myself together enough to pick up her dead babies, and I buried them under the trees.

There was sympathy from my mother of course, even my father shook his head, and Bob too, but there was no sympathy from one of the postmen when he arrived on his bike later that morning.

News travelled fast in Betws-y-Coed.

"Lost your pigs then," he said handing me a fist full of bills.

"She had them a night early by my reckoning," I said, "and she's killed the lot."

"Oh well they're funny things pigs you know," he laughed. "You never know what they'll get up to. If they don't want a litter that's the sort of thing they do you see," and with that he hopped on his bike.

"See you tomorrow," he said cheerfully. I could have kicked his spokes in. Everybody but everybody from bus drivers to postmen reckoned they knew more about pigs than I did, but after a few minutes it occurred to me that she could possibly have saved one or two and I went back and had a closer look. While she was in the yard I pulled the bedding out but there was nothing there and I chucked it back in disgust.

It was a bleak day. It rained incessantly. Lunch time we started to empty buckets and bowls in the lofts, crawling around on sore wet knees yet again through the curtains and damp cobwebs, until shouts from downstairs informed us that water had started to cascade through a skylight into the bar and we spent the rest of the afternoon dealing with that catastrophe by diverting water from a broken down-spout with odd lengths of drain pipe and even a length of rolled up lino.

You got used to being wet at the Waterloo.

That night, with the rain still dripping into a couple of buckets, the bar was full of gloom and no one sang that night until a few minutes before closing time. I felt so fed up I went to bed early and with the cellars in mind, read a book on breeding mushrooms.

In the morning, as I was on my way to open the petrol station my mother reminded me I hadn't fed the pig. I didn't need reminding. As far as I was concerned she could get her own breakfast.

"You must feed the poor thing," she said and after an hour or two I relented and went up to throw her a bucket, consoling myself that it would be one of the last. She was going to market. She'd be pork pies by the end of the week.

After I'd thrown the slops into the trough I was struck by the fact that she was still very quiet. Instead of trotting out to gobble it up, there was no sign of her.

A chill started to weave its way up my back. She could be dead. Not thinking what I was doing I passed a 'swill wet' hand through my hair. I'd have a hell of a job to sell her if she was dead, even for pork pies. I'd have to get to the market early and prop her up with a stick.

I strode over to the ark and lifted the sack.

She was lying on her side and as she looked up at me her whiskers twitched and she heaved a huge sigh.

I must have stood rooted to the spot for several minutes, struck absolutely dumb. I couldn't think or speak, I could only stand and stare. That incredible, wonderful beast had done something that was unbelievable. She'd had another litter. Guzzling away at her were ten more tiny pink piglets.

I just couldn't believe it, but there they were. She'd had twenty-one piglets over two nights.

CHAPTER 7

Doctor Bowden was the village doctor, a little old fashioned man with a vintage car, an Austin Twelve of the 1920's that he kept in a lop-sided tin shed with an electric light bulb strung under the bonnet to keep it warm.

After they're dead and gone, some men are said to have been in tune with the times, but I think Doctor Bowden was simply in tune with the place, or at least in tune with the place as he still saw it. His 1930's appearance, his white starched collars and little round wire framed spectacles, his slow and stooping gait and placid yet genial personality summed him up exactly. He was a corner stone in a village of two layers, a cosmopolitan community where many avoided wherever possible all contact with outsiders and politely but positively refused to awake from their pre-war identity.

As the village doctor, he treated tourists for cuts and bruises down at his riverside house, but they always looked out of place in that sombre brown waiting room, and although there had been tourists before the war, they'd never come in such enormous numbers as in the Sixties, arriving in never ending convoys of cars and day tripper coaches, and for some like Doctor Bowden, rich and penniless alike, this brash and noisy invasion was

97

transparent. The roadsweeper, bent over his broom and the widow pruning her roses may have heard them and felt their weight and number gathering around the wool shop, spilling into the road and blocking the Pont-y-Pair bridge to shout at the leaping salmon, but they really took no notice of such people.

For those people like Doctor Bowden, the village hadn't moved into the Fifties let alone the Sixties. For them the fishing was good, the salmon were still large and plentiful, there were water colours to finish, there was no television, but there were still countless hours of orchestral gramophone records to share, and forever aloof to the tourist trade they lived in a totally different world, a world I came to admire. For them the tourists simply bounced off the village like moths at the window, disappearing with the coming of winter without even having scratched the surface.

Of all the old people in Betws-y-Coed, Doctor Bowden and his wife stand out in my memory most of all because during the winter months I sometimes worked for them. Sometimes I was the odd-job man, sometimes the gardener, and for a week I was the doctor.

All the vintage trappings of a genteel and bygone existence were still in that big sombre house, a little faded and frayed at the edges perhaps but it was all there like a gallery of forgotten rooms in a museum, each room heavy with old fashioned furniture and dowdy lamp shades, and some like those rooms in the attic, crying out with the echoes of children, a box of books for boys in a corner and pictures of ballerinas still pinned to the walls, and downstairs in an ancient kitchen, a maid in a white apron could be found. A maid who would be hauling in coal scuttles one minute and rolling pastry the next on a bare bleached table.

This tiny spectacled teenage kid with the ear splitting laugh of a maniac and short cropped coal black hair and hands to match, must have been the worst maid ever to wear a pinny.

The daughter of a farmer, Margaret was a product of the age, who at the age of sixteen anyway had no time for the rigours of farming or the finesse of domestic service, but today many years later, she may be a raving beauty with a title and manners to match, and having witnessed her initial assault upon the world I would say it was quite possible.

Old Mrs Bowden was as deaf as a post, a tall and haughtily wafer-like figure who ran her house with a stern authority, but she was no match for Margaret.

For both the old doctor and his wife it was the end of an era, but there's no doubt at all that she felt it most, the days of domestic service were finished. She now had a maid who belonged to the anarchy of the Sixties, a teenager who laughingly shouted in retaliation the most outrageous things straight at her whenever her hearing aid was switched off and literally danced a jig after her, pulling faces barely a yard behind her as soon as her back was turned.

Mrs Bowden was so deaf you tended to shout at him too.

"It's my wife who's deaf," he'd say quietly.

During that first winter I'd been working for the coalman whilst waiting for the petrol station to be built. I enjoyed humping sacks of coal around. There was something very satisfying about it, but I was also the driver of the lorry and with the marvellous old Mr Hughes (another of my pig advisers) I used to drive the decrepit old wagon up to some of the loneliest farms imaginable, bouncing around on narrow roads and rocky tracks for miles on end, always climbing higher and higher.

Being so isolated they usually took a lorry load at a time, and invariably it was an assault course to get the sacks emptied into the bunker or the right shed. At one place you had to carry each sack up a dozen steps, and then do a 'knees bend' under the apple tree, but they were good times.

So often I remember sitting by hot and shiny black stoves glowing red in warm and friendly kitchens where heavy oak dressers stood laden with colourfully patterned china plates, and there we'd sit among the gleaming brasses swapping the gossip of the day, clutching mugs of steaming sweet tea and chunks of fruity home-made cake, and always there was a view from the window. That always stole me away as my companion old Mr Hughes chatted on in Welsh, and it's strange but I don't think I've ever known such peace of mind as I felt in those days, a feeling of sanctuary almost, to be with such friendly people who spoke a language I neither could nor wanted to break into.

I think it was the rather good fortune I'd had in steering the coal lorry that prompted old Doctor Bowden to ask me to drive his old green car.

The coal lorry should never have been on the road, steering it was like steering a ship. You had to start turning it into a bend long before you reached it, because for a while nothing happened, and having been amazed if not impressed that someone was mad enough to drive it, Doctor Bowden got me to deliver his pills and medicines to outlying patients, driving up through the forests to the same bleak tops of the moor land areas that I took the coal lorry to.

During dry spells, the old Austin could be driven as an open car and it went very well. The faster you went the colder it got of course and it was very heavy and cumbersome compared to a modern car, and changing gear was like stirring a barrel of tar, but at least by the time I arrived no-one needed to shake the bottle. The ringing sound of bottles dancing together on the dickie seat made it sound like a milk float.

Looking back on it, I don't know how useful I was to the old doctor but I think we were probably good for each other. I remember some afternoons we used to sit upstairs and shoot crows from the windows. The crows used to raid the fruit trees and everything else come to that, so we took to shooting them with a couple of ancient air rifles that he used to produce from a cupboard, a cupboard that I suspect was full of memories.

We had marvellous crow shooting competitions, he at one window and me at the next, scanning the sky like a couple of airborne gunners in a flying fortress.

"Here they come," he'd say suddenly.

"There are dozens of them!"

"I've got one!"

"Great!"

"He's going down!"

"Look out they're above you!"

"He's in the river!"

We'd sit up there all afternoon sometimes, talking and shooting, and he talked wistfully about life with such a gentle humour, but it was nearly always about the present and now I wish I'd been a bit more inquisitive about his past. I'm glad I met him, he hadn't long to go by then and there we were, one coming to the end of his journey, the other not even knowing where he was going.

The last time I saw him I was recovering from the flu and when he got to the top of the stairs he looked terrible, and as he sat down for a breather he said we'd got it all wrong, that he should be the patient and I should be doing the visiting.

He was such a good listener though, especially during our shooting days, he always wanted to know about the younger generation's opinion, and during one period he was very interested in the play I was writing. When at last I was ready to unleash it upon the world he provided all the music for it, music for the overture, the creepy bits, even for the intervals, all chosen from his vast collection of seventy-eights.

We spent an entire day selecting that music and the play was only a thriller. I called it "Wind of Fear". Margaret the maid pinned a poster up in the waiting room and one of the patients complained about it.

Mrs Bowden who was normally such a serious person thought that the words "Wind of Fear" pinned up in her husband's waiting room was so funny. She groped her way to a kitchen chair and leaned on the table with her head in her hands, the tears streaming down her face. She just couldn't stop laughing.

Margaret and I couldn't understand why she thought it was so funny and Margaret stood behind her saying she'd really gone crackers now, but today all these years later I think I understand. It really was the end for them.

Mrs Bowden didn't come to see the play when at last we put it on at the village hall, but he did on both nights. So did many other people, in fact the place was full.

I can't quite recall how that play came into being, I suppose it was due to something said in a crowded bar. It's dreadful when you count up the disasters that originate in crowded bars.

Looking back on it I expect it sprang from the fact that with no television to dull the senses, I'd helped with the Dulyn Amateur Dramatic Society further down the valley at Tal-y-Bont and someone on a bar stool said, "Why don't we put on a few plays here?" and I suppose to keep the cost down I said I would write something. What I do remember quite vividly however, is wishing some weeks later that I had never started on it as I'd also become the producer, but by now, I was getting to be as crazy as the rest of them.

The problem was that no one could learn their lines. Rehearsals that had started with so much enthusiasm with several rounds being bought in the bar before starting, were now becoming an ordeal. It's true it was a full three act play, it's true too that it lasted the best part of two hours and it's also true that none of the cast had ever been in a play before, but I thought it was going to be easy. It was after all beautifully written and no one therefore should have had trouble remembering hauntingly beautiful lines like "Crumbs he's dead," and "I never did it constable," but after a couple of months it was quite clear that we were getting nowhere.

Then the ghost gave up. She only had half a dozen lines too and in stepped my mother. There was no other way of filling the gap and she said her public demanded it.

Somehow or other the show had to go on. I'd paid the printer for the posters. Clearly it was time for a big decision. Something had to be done.

The remedy was inspirational to say the very least. I decided to record them reading it, and I put it on with them miming to the recording.

The response to my brain wave was one of distinct uncertainty.

"You won't have to learn your lines," I told them, "it will all be pre-recorded."

After Williams the Pru, an Insurance Agent who played the solicitor, had bought another round of drinks their faces began to light up, and the prompter went home.

Peter Dodd who played the corpse extremely well, had a tape recorder which he used for playing non-stop music in his restaurant, and one night the cast assembled in one of the Waterloo's more acceptable bedrooms, one with a carpet to avoid too much echo, and we read through it, pausing wherever necessary to allow for theatrical business like the opening of a book and various bits that needed dramatic silences.

After a while, and the re-doing of certain bits, it no longer sounded as if we were reading and it started to sound terrific. Mrs Williams Elsi Cottage was superb as the suspect wife, especially when she was on the right page, and Williams the Pru was going from strength to strength, but it took ages to get it all on tape. It was nearly closing time by the time we finished, but as we all sat together in the bar that night we thought we were going to be a great success.

Rehearsals from then on of course were very different. It was no longer a matter of remembering the words, it was now a matter of remembering what to do with them. There were all sorts of new problems, most of the time the words coming from the tape were saying things like, 'the view from this window is magnificent,' while the owner of the voice was still hanging up his coat, but eventually after another couple of nights it started to gel. The words and the actions were beginning to synchronise and the most surprising thing was that without further study, we suddenly all knew our lines which gave us a great deal of confidence. Nevertheless, we still mimed it.

When it came to the first night, the confidence failed to show up, and so too did 'scoop' Thomas of the Weekly News as he was known, but I think only because there wasn't a bus from Llanrwst that would get him there in time. He really was a wonderfully unhurried reporter, but instead the paper sent a fidgety woman who came by car and announced herself as the chief drama critic, and that was a shame. The audience seemed to enjoy it, but I think the poor woman who came all the way from Colwyn Bay, failed to grasp what was actually going on, even though before the overture I went out before the curtain to explain this was a 'first' in theatrical history.

I stood there under a spotlight tightening the belt of my very theatrical red dressing gown, and explained exactly the technique of producing this world première so that there could be no accusations of cheating. Not that I needed to, the whole village had known about it for weeks. The format was so simple, even my mother and Mrs Williams had grasped it. Everything but everything was on tape, the whole show, non-stop.

Once we'd got the words onto a big main reel we'd added the creepy music, splicing it in at all the appropriate spots, and we'd been so pleased with the result, that we went the whole hog, adding the overture, the music for both the intervals, and all the sound effects such as various cars arriving and the thunder at the end of the play.

There was no doubt about it, it was an extremely efficient method of production. The only problem was keeping up with the damn thing. Once the wires to the loudspeakers were connected and the 'play' button was pressed you were off. During rehearsals it had been fine, but now it was like being dragged along by an express train. The slightest hitch backstage meant a desperate race to catch up. There was no allowance for any sort of delay. Even the intervals were a disaster. They were over before the audience were back in their seats!

It sounded good enough, both the music and the dialogue, with the words coming from two loudspeakers hidden under the furniture, and we'd learnt that it wasn't necessary to open and close our mouths too much in order to mine effectively, all that was needed was a little mouth movement and the occasional gesture.

It was however, from the very first moment the tape machine was switched on, pure hell.

Waiting for the overture to finish was agony. Waiting in the dark behind the scenery, nerves were like bow strings with Aneurin going purple and Williams the Pru handing round a flask of whiskey and then feverishly trying to get it back for another swig before the curtain went up.

I was at the top of the stairs. After my speech I'd given Peter the signal to switch on, and now Mrs Williams and

I were up on the landing keeping out of sight so that when the curtain went up the audience would first see an empty sitting room.

I was playing the young doctor. It was a very good part of course and the action opened with us coming down the stairs. The doctor, having just examined her ailing husband, played by Pete, who was supposed to be ill in bed.

As we stood just out of sight at the top of the stairs though, waiting for the end of the overture, I had to keep whispering to Mrs Williams to calm down, she was shaking like a jelly. I kept telling her that everything was under control.

"It's alright," I kept whispering, "everything will be just as its been in rehearsals. Don't panic, just do the same as you've been doing for weeks. Everything's OK."

She took a number of deep breaths and I clutched reassuringly at the stethoscope hanging round my neck.

The music stopped at last, the curtain went up with a rush and with a push in the back, I launched Mrs Williams down the stairs upon her short acting career.

I paused for a second before following her entrance while she spoke her opening line.

"Thank you for coming doctor," she said, and I started to follow, tugging reassuringly again at the belt of my dressing gown.

Dressing Gown!! I still had my dressing gown on!! The tape ran on.

"Do you think there's any improvement in him doctor?" she asked looking back up the stairs, puzzled that I hadn't yet followed her.

All she saw of course was a whirlwind up on the landing ripping off its dressing gown.

"Oh I think so," my voice said casually from the loudspeakers, as I *raced* down the stairs to join her.

They were pretty tough were the members of that cast. Most people would never have gone through it a second time, but stoically we did the two nights we said we'd do.

Twice Mrs Williams forgot her entrance cues and found her voice on stage long before she was, and in one performance someone couldn't find an all important book but nevertheless found himself saying, "Ah, here it is," and in another part of the play someone dropped a cup of tea, and as the recording didn't make allowances for accidents, all he could do was smartly back-heel it under the sofa.

By now the audience was in stitches, and on the second night the great dramatic end to the play was completely ruined by my mother and Mrs Williams arguing over when to drop the curtain.

The previous night they'd dropped it just a little bit too early.

"Let the first two peels of thunder rip through," I told

them, "And then as the third quieter rumble starts, let it come down ever so slowly, so that by the time the thunder's died away, the curtain's down."

"Ah yes of course," they said together, realising their mistake, which of course had ruined my dramatic stance. It was after all a very telling moment. I, the young doctor and leading character, had realised at the climax of the story that the old man hadn't died by natural causes, instead he'd died by the hand of some supernatural power, and stunned by the realisation of this, I stood staring like a statue, mortified by absolute horror.

On that second, and definitely last night, I acted that realisation of horror sweeping over me superbly. The thunder ripped through the room, the curtains at the French window billowed in the wind and I stood rooted to the spot. Along came the second great clap of thunder. It was terrific and now for the next rumble of thunder. Gradually it started to arrive.

It arrived, and soon it went. It had gone and the curtain hadn't budged. I held the dramatic stance and still the curtain didn't come down.

Behind the scenery I could hear them arguing.

"There's another clap of thunder."

"No it's gone."

I spoke through clenched teeth, "Let it down."

Still nothing happened, "Let it down." I repeated but

they took no notice. Still they argued.

"There's another clap of thunder," my mother was saying.

"No there are only three," Mrs Williams was saying.

"For God's sake let it down," I hissed, and at long last it very slowly started to fall. By the time it was down the audience had their coats on.

I don't know what we were celebrating but we had a good party that night, and we all vowed to keep off the stage and stay on the beer.

I suppose however, that it must have been on the strength of my performance that I became a real doctor.

A few weeks later Doctor Bowden wasn't well again, and he sent for me one weekend and sitting up in bed he outlined his plan.

"I'm not getting up for morning surgery next week," he said, "You can do it."

I looked at him for a moment thinking he might be delirious.

"No I mean it," he said, "I might get up for the evening surgery but you can do the mornings."

So I became a doctor for a week.

It worked very well too. His plan was ingeniously simple. I sat at his desk down in the surgery and just asked each patient a few questions, any sort of questions that came into my head really, like, "What's wrong with you then?" and while the patient explained, I wrote whatever notes I thought necessary onto a sheet of paper. When I felt that I'd jotted down enough facts like, "He's got a pain in his shoulder … Can't move fingers … Can't bend elbow … Yells when I squeeze it, " I just had to add his name, age and address and hand the bit of paper to Margaret, who invariably was standing chewing gum by my chair, for her to take it up to old Doctor Bowden. He then read the notes, made out a prescription and Margaret brought it down. It was easy, it was just a case of finish with one patient and in with the next.

You would never realise though, how enthralling it is for a doctor to shout "Next!" You just haven't a clue what else you're going to get.

All week I squeezed elbows and knees, some in nylons, gazed with fascination up nostrils and deep in eardrums with that little torch thing, and explored people's mouths and throats while holding down their tongue with a lolly stick, and all the time – making detailed notes like – tongue covered in white stuff, funny little wobbly thing at the back, very red.

Margaret didn't find it very interesting. She spent most of her time looking under the furniture for more chewing gum, but I was absolutely fascinated. The things people told me when she was upstairs. I came to the conclusion that at least 25% of household accidents are caused by events they don't actually come straight out with.

I don't think many people thought I was a real doctor, certainly not those who knew me of course, but it worked.

I did however have one worry.

"What do I do if I get a woman who thinks she is pregnant?" I asked after that first morning.

Old Doctor Bowden paused for a moment and then sliding under the covers he just said, "Oh you'll think of something."

CHAPTER 8

It was a hard life when winter came to the Waterloo and every winter I tried another bedroom. There were after all plenty to choose from. I always hoped to find a warmer one but I never managed it. Walking into any of the bedrooms in that place was like entering a deep freeze, and of course it was worse in winter.

If you tried to warm your room up with an electric heater it had such an alarming effect upon the cold air that you needed fog lamps to find the door, in fact it was healthier to give up the heating and go to bed fully dressed. Many were the times I went to bed at the Waterloo with gloves and a scarf on, and if it hadn't tickled so much I would have persevered with the balaclava helmet.

I must admit though, when the snow came and spread its muffling blanket over everything, it was incredibly beautiful. We had a lot of snow in those days and when it came down thick, pretty well everything came to a stop for days, and it was so still and quiet. The old hotel looked like a picture in a sketch pad and to this day I can see it in my mind's eye, its bleak grey mass draped in thick snow against the green and splattered white of the pine forest rising in the background.

Every winter the joints of water pipes by the hundred,

oozed apart to reveal pencils of frozen water. We did our own plumbing most of the time and our joints always seemed to let us down, but between them too, whole lengths of pipe would bulge and split with the promise of a watery grave once the thaw set in.

I've never seen a place like it for water pipes. They were enormous, they intertwined around the building like a tangle of rigid spaghetti, and in a sort of workshop area at the back door, some of the great stop-cocks could always be relied on to jam, usually in the open position.

If you ever think of sawing through a pipe that's bursting to explode with extremely cold and angry high-pressure water, forget it. Instead do anything to turn off the stop cock, lever it, hammer it, plead with it even, but unless you want to be drowned in a jet of freezing water, don't use that hacksaw.

When the thaw came, as it usually did by August, you needed people on every landing not only hollering frenzied instructions down to the back door, but of course relaying the answers back up again.

"Turn it off!" someone upstairs would shout first, and on the floor below someone would pass it on.

"Turn it off!" "Turn it off!" and so on, and with a torrent flooding down the stairs, the reply would be passed up on its return journey.

"Which one?"

"Which one?"

"Which one?"

There were pipes everywhere, not only under the floorboards where you would expect to find a few, but up the walls and even down the staircases, and when you think of the dry rot there, it was probably only the plumbing that was keeping the place together, but it was nothing less than a nightmare trying to sort out which pipe, among dozens disappearing up through the ceiling, connected with any of the hundreds of others on the floor above.

We'd had a good warning however of the Waterloo's plumbing. Just before we moved in I found a massive pressure gauge mounted on a water pipe about four inches thick down in one of the cellars. It was a most impressive thing. It was like the big glass fronted dial Scottish engineers tap with a podgy finger down in the engine room, and blowing off the cobwebs I peered at the indicator hand.

"Nil pressure," I said.

"Of course there's no pressure," my father said, "All the water's turned off."

I tapped the dial. Nothing happened. I tapped it again and very slowly it keeled over backwards and a plume of water four inches thick smashed me back against the wall.

We must have come close to sinking that building. I

117

remember once I was repairing a pipe in a first floor bedroom immediately above the telephone which was in the front bar. It was situated in a wooden cupboard next to the fireplace, a cream painted booth so small it had to have ventilation holes in the ceiling.

We'd been at it all day and were losing the battle. As soon as we mended one burst, another unleashed itself upon us, and my father decided at last to call in help from a plumber. It was just unfortunate that as he stepped into the phone booth and closed the door, I unscrewed a connector in the water pipe just above the ventilation holes.

It wouldn't have been too bad for him if he hadn't pulled off the door handle in his efforts to get out.

A similar fate happened one morning to a woman who came in looking for a toilet.

My father and Bob had been building a new ladies toilet block down the passage from the back bar. Nothing too posh or expensive of course, just the sort of thing you'd expect to find in any refugee camp, and somehow or other, although they thought they'd finished, in one of the breeze block cubicles the cistern wasn't screwed to the wall.

They'd used big old cast iron cisterns, salvaged I think from the ruins of the coach house and the stables, the type that was suspended high above your head with a good long chain to pull.

The lady carelessly chose to use the one that was only

held aloft by the pipe that connected it to the lavatory pan, but to be fair to her, she was obviously high class because she pulled the chain.

She said so when she emerged. In rather a dazed sort of voice and dripping all over the carpet she said, "I pulled the chain."

I could see she was absolutely drenched, her hair was plastered flat all over her face, and leaving her standing there I went and had a quick look and I could see the cistern had tipped forward and was now completely empty.

I didn't really know what to do with her, she was still just standing there dripping all over the carpet, so I offered to see if I could find her a hair dryer, which of course wouldn't have got her clothes dry, but then unfortunately Bob, realising something was up, rose tottering to his feet from behind the bar where he'd been stocking up the shelves.

She was stunned I suppose by all that cold water, but I thought I was beginning to get through to her when Bob at last thought of something to say. He was standing scratching his head and swaying backwards and forwards while I was asking her in words of one syllable and speaking very slowly, if she would like a cup of tea, when in a slurred attempt to be helpful he offered to take her clothes away.

I don't know where she went with all those wet clothes

on, but she suddenly walked out.

"Thas awful Nox," Bob said disapprovingly. "Fancy going out looking like that."

I used to get pretty wet and cold myself even before the petrol station was built, when I worked one winter for a local builder. In spite of the arctic conditions I had to sit out in the open on the lorry that picked me up in the morning because the cab was always full. I think even Jock had someone on his lap by the way he drove.

We were putting an extra storey on the lecture rooms alongside Plas-y-Brennin, the Outdoor Activity Centre at Capel Curig, and the snow gathered so thick on the tarpaulins we'd erected over them, that the whole thing collapsed one night with several upright scaffolding poles going straight through the floor below, missing only by a few feet several of the girls who were sleeping down there.

I've never known it to be so cold, the milk was freezing in the bottles and splitting them wide open, and as we worked to untangle the wreckage of that night, our fingers felt as if they were dropping off. The tarpaulins were like sheets of iron and the ropes and their knots were frozen solid.

In the end you got acclimatised to the cold at Betws-y-Coed and when I look back on the way John Godbert and I used to go canoeing, I don't even remember being cold, with perhaps one exception when I fell out and was swept half a mile down the River Conway from Beaver Pool before I was able to grab the branch of an overhanging tree, but that was a day between Christmas and New Year, when the river was swollen by snow.

Little of our canoeing was done during the summer because of avoiding the fishing season, and I can't help thinking that the way lads cocoon themselves in special warm suits these days is a bit soft. They even wear crash helmets now, but when John and I used to go down the waterfall above Beaver Pool we didn't even have a life jacket. We just used a car's inner tube.

We never needed two of anything because we only had the one canoe, his bendy old canvas kayak, and we just took it in turns, and when it was a flight down that waterfall we used to tie the inner tube around each other's shoulders with a bit of string.

The knack of shooting into Beaver Pool was to stay upright at all cost, and then if the spray cover held fast and no water came in while you were submerged, you rose, eyes open, to the surface like an ascending submarine. It was like being in slightly green sparkling lemonade.

We acquired a proper buoyancy thing one day from Alan Hughes who used to run an Outdoor Activity Centre up the Lledr Valley. He saw us at it from the road and he gave us a life jacket.

"For goodness sake you two," he said. "Have this on

us."

One of the best things to emerge during those winters at the Waterloo however was the indoor hockey. It started one Christmas with my young cousin David stuffing some rags into a small plastic net which I think had held an assortment of nuts, and with the ingenuity of any kid hell-bent on total destruction, he started to whack it around the ballroom with a walking stick. Before long he'd found another stick for me and we were racing up and down between the tables and chairs trying to score goals against each other in the fireplaces at either end of the room.

Sometime in the New Year when the tables and chairs had been cleared away, we involved a few from the bar one night and it grew immediately from that, only with a proper ball, and by the end of the week there were dozens at it, even rules were being drawn up and whole teams of grown men, especially some I played football with, were charging around that room hacking each other to bits. People were far more active in those days.

Being the Waterloo of course it was an extremely large ballroom and every winter from then on it became famous for its indoor hockey, or at least the unsophisticated mayhem we called hockey (you could whack the ball with both sides of the stick), but the fascinating thing about its growth, was the almost cultish search for the perfect stick. Clumsy walking sticks very soon disappeared from the scene and instead players made their own from the branches of trees, all with different angles and twists to suit the individual. Some had curved sticks for devious winkling in tight corners, some with angled bottoms to lift the ball, some had sticks of ultra lightweight for speed, and some had heavyweight sticks for bloody-mindedness.

Some days you'd look out the window about dusk, and you'd see someone trudging through the snow carrying home a bundle of branches cut from the forest, and he'd come in and over a pint show off his hopes for the ultimate weapon, and such was the competition that before long, if you asked where he'd found such a promising batch of sticks, he wouldn't tell you.

Competition was pretty keen on the football field too. Rivalry between local footballs clubs had to be seen to be believed, and it wasn't safe to see it from the touch line either. Twice I saw referees set upon and linesmen thrown in the river and the hooligans weren't kids in those days, they were adults, and up at Penmachno many of the most aggressive types were women.

At Penmachno, the pitch sloped so much up the side of the mountain, the left winger needed climbing boots, and some years earlier when playing for Colwyn Bay I'd suffered the worst verbal attack of my life there when I tackled, for the first time, one of their half backs.

"Can't you see, you B------ he's only got one eye!"

Immediately upon closer inspection I saw this was true. He only had one eye and yet he was as quick and skilful as anyone else on the pitch, but dare you tackle him? Not unless you first asked permission from the home crowd.

At half time there on another occasion, our outside right showed the referee the bruises on his shoulder.

"Who's doing that?" the referee asked, "that number four?"

"Is it Hell" the winger said. "It's that woman with the umbrella."

Our ground at Betws was typical of its day. We changed upstairs above the Royal Oak stables. It was filthy, the lavatory hadn't seen water since the horses were there, and when it rained the spectators sheltered under a giant oak tree.

In those days though, the game was played by men of all ages, unlike today when it seems to be played by boys, and in those days there were loads of supporters. Village teams were supported by whole communities and there were always two coaches going from Betws-y-Coed to away matches, one for the team and supporters, the other entirely for supporters.

There were so many great characters in the game then, some of them now already dead, but in those days nothing but nothing took pride of place to the fixtures of the league. Mel Humphries, a forester with arms thicker than some mens legs and captain of the Betws team, played on his wedding day and brought the game to a halt with both teams falling about with laughter when he got hit by the ball in a place you wouldn't choose *any* day let alone on your wedding day, but no one would miss a match for anything, and that Betws side in the magpie shirts was a great team.

Among them we had a young farmer, Gordon Breeze, the best centre forward I've ever played alongside who got an injury and died of tetanus; our amateur international goalkeeper Gerry Pierce who was in goal for Wales; George Kennedy a stocky little ginger haired Liverpudlian who just didn't know how to stop running; and Jennings the bank clerk who I once saw squirm with the ball through the entire Llanrwst team and send them crashing out of the cup with a goal so incredible I'll never forget it as long as I live.

After a few years, when I was getting a bit long in the tooth, Les Williams and I moved on to another team run by another ex Betws player 'Hard Nut Cecil'. This was 'Gwydir Forest' at the Forestry School, not so much a school but a wooden hut prison camp for lumberjacks, and that first season was a disaster. We lost one match at Llanfairfechan 20 – Nil and that week the newspaper headline read 'Forest Axed'.

As players they were far more lumberjacks than

footballers and I think most of the goals we conceded in that first season were from free kicks and penalties, but gradually we reorganised the defence, getting them to stop punching people as they passed, and then miraculously the following season everything changed. We suddenly had a brilliant team.

It just happened that the new intake included players with a lot of experience, some having failed trials with clubs like Nottingham Forest, and wherever else there were woods, and our new centre half had once actually played for Grimsby which, believe it or not, bestowed upon us invaluable prestige.

During that next season no one could believe it. We were now so good and winning a lot of matches, the other clubs were getting rattled.

Teams that had beaten us easily were now running into a brick wall, and the draw at Llanfairfechan was so fiercely contested that afterwards the referee, with the opposition's manager and chairman to back him up, burst into our dressing room as we sat there soaking in big tin baths, and declared he was reporting every single one of us to the league. Admittedly it had been a bit rough and a couple of their team were in hospital, but as the row went on and insult was hurled after insult, I couldn't help thinking it was somewhat ironic. At exactly the same fixture only twelve months before, in exactly the same dressing room, the door had crashed open in just the same way and the referee backed up by the opposition's manager and chairman, had commended the whole team on a 'thoroughly sporting performance' as he put it, but then of course we'd lost 20 – Nil.

What a difference a year makes. We were now on top of the world, and very nearly on top of the league. As we walked from the ground people booed and little kids threw stones. At last we'd earned some respect.

I often wonder what happened to some of those fellers. Most were eventually scattered around the British Isles and some went abroad, and I don't suppose any are playing football or 'Waterloo hockey' anymore, but the most surprising character to play 'Waterloo hockey' was an Australian who booked in with his wife one winter afternoon and who went out walking every day in the snow with no socks on. He just wore sandals.

Naturally we thought this was a bit strange, but he was a good hockey player. He was soon joining in and mixing it with the roughest.

Being in the depth of winter, they were the only residents we'd had for weeks, and they sat round the fire with everyone, happily sharing rounds and joking about this and that, and then one night he asked me if I might know of a cottage they might come and rent in the summer because he had some writing to finish.

"What are you writing?" I asked.

"It's a book about athletics," he said.

"Any particular events?" I asked.

"The mile," he said.

… And I said "What do you know about the mile then?"

Someone was handing him a drink, and at that moment, all I heard was that he'd always been interested in it.

It was a couple of days later when someone recognised him and we looked again at the visitors book. It was Herb Elliot, one of the greatest milers of all time, a world record holder, and right there and then the current holder of the Olympic Gold Medal!

No wonder no amount of battering he got playing 'Waterloo hockey' tired him out, and they stayed on for the rest of the week too.

To think – I'd asked him what he knew about the mile!

One of the leading local exponents of our hockey matches however was Pete Dodd. This incurable eccentric who, with the first fall of snow used to go ski-ing on a couple of floorboards, actually managed to introduce an element of style to the game. This he did by starting a craze for 'ornamented' sticks.

I think everyone had started to wrap some sort of binding around the handles, but Pete took it much further of course, actually carving designs on his best ones. I remember he took a whole day once decorating a special lightweight 'dribbler' as he called it, and in the first five minutes of desperate dribbling that night, it was smashed to smithereens.

The shouts and screams of agony used to echo all the way down to the bar, and that of course is where we all used to end up, some earlier than others.

The most select place to meet your friends at the time though, and after all, that is what drinking is all about, was behind the curtain at Pete's place. Peter only had a restaurant licence over the river at Ty Gwyn, and he eventually lost that for a while, but anyone in the know, knew that by the witching hour it was open house at Doddies, but behind that curtain there was never room for more than about a dozen people.

Ty Gwyn was a remarkable place, about as dilapidated as the Waterloo, where the most generous mountains of exquisite food were served up in a musty jungle of antiques and theatrical props, and in front of the bar he hung a huge thick red curtain that could be drawn closed no more than a couple of feet from the counter. It hung from the ceiling to the floor and late at night, if you could find your way in (in the dark) and then find the gap somewhere in the middle of the curtain, you'd stick your head in and see who was hiding there.

It was always a magic moment, for you creeping in and

of course for those already behind the curtain. Imagine it, it's late at night, the door was never locked, you've let yourself in, groped your way in the dark through a couple of rooms, bumped cursing into a couple of tables, a grandfather clock, the harp or that blasted gong, and behind the curtain there's a dozen people being absolutely quiet wondering who you are, or more to the point, wondering if it's the police.

In those wee small illegal hours, there were some marvellous stories told, and presiding over it all was the Duchess, Doddy's mother. I can still hear that wonderful laugh, hoarse and smoky, and I can see her too, seated behind the bar in a regal gown and giant sparklers. A 70 year old 'theatrical' dame who received countless proposals and made sure that we all knew about them.

Ellis Hughes proposed to her the first day he collected the pig bin. I don't know which one died first but his proposals went on for years, and on those clandestine nights, when the chance of a police raid served only to enhance the game, Ellis Hughes' horse and cart parked outside was a dead give-away.

Whenever he was squeezed in behind that curtain, there was a chance the sergeant might rumble us. That wouldn't have mattered too much, but to a passing police car it would have stood out like a sore thumb. Cruising down the A5 they weren't likely to be aroused by a car or two outside a restaurant and guest house after midnight, but a horse and cart was just asking for trouble.

He couldn't care less of course, they'd already had him for having no lights so he'd stuck candles on the cart and gone to the police station and told them that's all they were getting, but one night while he was there at Ty Gwyn, someone nipped out and pinched it, leading the old horse up the road and once out of ear shot, walloping it on the rump and sending both horse and cart rattling off at a gallop.

When he came back in the rest of us were talking, but I saw him whisper something to the Duchess and she laughed so much it nearly killed her. Eventually she whispered it to somebody else and they passed it on until we all knew except old Ellis who was still telling one of his stories.

As practical jokes go however, it was a complete failure. When I left it was getting on for 2.00 a.m. but some of them were still there, and so was the horse. It was standing there with its cart in the kerb again, having stopped and turned around in the middle of the road, it had come back for him.

That was a memorable occasion for another reason, because back in the Waterloo that night, I again heard the footsteps.

I was mostly there on my own that winter. My parents

were away on holiday and once the barman had gone home I was the sole occupant.

That night I found the embers of the fire in one of the bars were still glowing with a promise of life, and seeing as someone had left a newspaper in an armchair, I poked some warmth into the fire and sat down with the dogs at my feet for a quick read before going to bed.

We all knew the Waterloo was haunted but just how exactly, or by what or by whom, we never did discover. Several of the cleaners had been terrified by unaccountable footsteps on landings, and once, I myself had experienced exactly that on the fourth floor of the tower block. It was in that part of the building we hadn't yet 'tamed' and on that occasion I was plastering over holes in the wall of a derelict bedroom, when I heard someone coming down the hall. There were no carpets up there.

We'd borrowed so many floorboards there were no floors in some rooms. It was completely bare and echoey, and when the footsteps got almost to the bedroom door I said - "In here Wendy," thinking it was the girl in the snack bar who'd promised to bring me a cup of coffee. However, it wasn't Wendy. The footsteps halted as soon as I spoke, and when I went to investigate there was no one there.

It was so totally baffling, and down in the snack bar, Wendy, with her nose in a book, jumped up as soon as I walked in, having forgotten me. She hadn't been upstairs and neither had anyone else because we were the only two there.

However, that late night when I was sitting reading the paper I was completely alone, and when the floorboards above started to creak, I remember thinking absent-mindedly to myself that it was only someone going to the toilet. I took no more notice than that. I sat there reading something that had caught my attention and it wasn't until the dogs started to growl that I put the paper down and looked up at the ceiling. The footsteps were slowly and creakily moving along the passage-way over my head, and it suddenly dawned on me. I was supposed to be on my own.

As I jumped up the dogs erupted ferociously into action and they raced up the stairs barking frantically, but although those two dogs and I searched that floor from one end to the other, we never saw a living soul. We looked under beds, in cupboards and in wardrobes but there was nothing there, nothing at all.

Nothing that is, that could be seen.

CHAPTER 9

The night of the 'Hiss and Boom' is a Waterloo story that is easy for me to tell, it lives on in my memory as plain as if it happened only a night ago, but it's another story that is impossible to explain, and to this day it remains a mystery.

If ever a building lived and breathed, groaned, murmured and whispered to you in the dead of night, it was the Waterloo.

The winter snows had only just gone, the days were suddenly mild, murky and damp, and I was still sleeping there alone. Early in the week, trade was very slow. Wendy in the snack bar read and knitted all day, and out in the petrol station I dozed with a book by the electric fire, while in the bar you might get no more than a dozen customers in at lunch time and not many more in the evening sometimes.

A lot of people had said they wouldn't sleep there alone for anything, but I felt it had no malice for me. I could walk the corridors late at night and feel no obsession to look over my shoulder, but one night, when I was sleeping as soundly as ever, something woke me up. At first I didn't know what had woken me, but one moment I'd been sound asleep, the next I was wide awake.

At that time my bedroom was right at the end overlooking the petrol station, and as I lay there in the silence of that great building, I gradually became aware of a 'heart beat'.

For a fleeting moment it had seemed to be there, then it seemed to be nothing more than something in my imagination, but lying on my back absolutely still, I strained my ears to pick up the slightest sound, and slowly, very slowly, I had to admit to myself that there was something in the air.

I think once I'd come to terms with that, I heard it more regularly. Perhaps it was growing louder I don't know, but every few moments there came the sound of a soft muffled 'boom'.

It was so very faint but it was there.

I got up, turned on the light, pulled on my shoes and looked at my watch. It was just after 3.00 a.m. I turned off the light and quietly pulled aside one of the curtains.

Outside nothing stirred. Whatever this noise was, it was definitely on the inside with me. You could somehow feel it, and when I opened the door and ventured out onto the landing, it was a little louder.

I stood there for some minutes and studied it. Strangely perhaps it hadn't started the dogs barking but there was something else with it now, something I hadn't heard before stepping out from the bedroom. Between each faint and reverberating 'boom', there was another sound, something that sounded like a 'hiss'.

Whatever it was, it was far off in that huge building, but I couldn't tell if it was high up or below ground. It didn't come down the passage like a sound at all, it was coming softly through everything, walls and doors, the ceiling and the floor. You couldn't tell how far away it was but it had that indefinable feeling of great weight behind it. It wasn't in the next room or the one beyond that, and beyond the landing I was on, the electricity had been turned off, so I went back for my torch.

I tried it and thankfully it worked, and having pulled on another sweater I crept along the landing, cringing and freezing to the spot every time I stepped on a creaky board. Whatever was causing the noise I didn't want to frighten it away. I was fascinated by it, *drawn* to it in fact.

Passing the tiny room where my mother prepared the early morning teas in the summer, I reached the end of that passage and I knew all too well that once into the next section, there would be no lights to switch on if the torch failed.

Here at last, the distant noise was distinct. It was louder and clearer and it was without question a 'hiss and boom', but where was it coming from? It was ridiculous. It sounded like the hiss of a giant snake and the booming of a deep sounding gong, and for a while, as I crept steadily onward, I began to think it was down in the cellars, but by the time I'd reached a landing on the main staircase, it was much louder and definitely coming from above with a vibration now following every boom.

I stood for a moment by a window in the pale yellow light of a street lamp below, and then slowly, I started to climb the next flight of stairs.

The floors above were those without carpets, there were no furnishings of any sort. Up there it was a bare and empty shell.

The torch started to flicker. I stopped and shook it back to life and started to climb again, but as I crept on, clutching the torch with one hand and the banister with the other, I gradually realised the vibration was becoming less pronounced. The hiss and boom was still as loud but the vibration was becoming less noticeable and it dawned on me that I was on the wrong course.

The noise was coming from the 'back' staircase. This was a little narrow stairway that climbed independently at the back of the hotel, up through the great central tower to the old staff quarters, spread out along the attics, all now empty and forgotten, and when I opened the door that led to those dusty old stairs, the noise *rushed* down at me.

'Hissssssss…..   Booooooom….. Hissssssss….. Booooooom…..'

I shook the torch again and started to climb.

At the top of that flight there was another door. This led onto the next floor and when I opened it, the noise grew even louder. There was no question now, I was on the right track.

There were five floors in that block and at the top of every flight of stairs there was a door, and every time I opened one, the noise was louder, *much* louder.

At last I was going up the final flight. The noise and the vibration was enormous. The old brown banister beneath my hand was shaking, the bare boards beneath my feet shuddered with every 'Booooom'.

The wavering little beam of my torch came to rest on the last door. I was at the top of the tower.

I twisted the little brass handle and pushed it open.

The noise was *deafening!* Each long drawn out ''HISSSSSSSSS' flooded my ears, as did the enormous deep and reverberating 'BOOOOOOOM'. It was deafening and almost paralysing, but as I stood on that top floor I realised at last where the noise was coming from.

There were several rooms up there, but my torch was trained on one door in particular. Water was splashing out from under it.

It was the door of a little room that held the water tank, a massive great tank of water with huge slate sides and whatever was making that noise was on the other side of that door.

I took hold the door knob and pulled the door open.

As long as I live, I'll never forget what I saw in the light of my torch. The water in the great tank had gone *crazy!* It was rushing in a tidal wave from one end to the other, climbing in a huge white tipped breaker high up the wall at one end, and then crashing back and sweeping across to climb up the wall on the other side.

I stood there amazed. Every time it rushed past from the right, the giant ball-cock fell and allowed a great plume of water to rush in from the big feed pipe with a terrific 'HIIIIIISSSSSSSS', and as the great wave swept back again it shot the ball-cock up with such a force, the sudden shutting off of the water produced a shattering 'BOOOOOMMMMMM'.

I just couldn't believe it. It just swept backwards and forwards, rushing from one side to the other. It was perpetual motion, it was just going on and on, 'HIIIIIIISSSSSSSSS . . . . . BOOOOOMMMMMM. HIIIIIISSSSSSSSS . . . . . BOOOOOMMMMMM'.

I had to stop it and there was only one way to do it. I pulled off my sweater and leant over the side. Holding my breath, I hung onto the ball-cock and, with each passing wave trying to pull me away, I managed to hold it up in the closed position until gradually the waves started to subside.

When at last the water was flat and still, I was able to

let go and for a while I remained leaning over the tank. I was very wet and very cold, but I knew that night I'd seen something that I would never be able to explain. Something, *something* had made hundreds of gallons of water go absolutely berserk.

CHAPTER 10

One day Don the postman slid down the roof and we discovered how Bob got drunk every morning.

Bob's deteriorating physical and mental condition between breakfast and lunch every day was something we put down to natural ability. By elevenses he was always capable of going to sleep and it took a great deal of persuasion to keep him upright, in fact only my father could do it with any measure of success. He somehow managed to fire him with enthusiasm, whereas anyone else would have just fired him.

Bob's morning tipple apparently was accomplished by draining the last liquid ounces from the variety of empty spirit bottles that were thrown in the 'empties' bin under the bar counter. After a busy night there would be plenty of them, and he must have held a few back each morning for quieter periods, probably round the back of the bar in the old pre-war kitchens. Out there, where he stacked the crates and empty barrels it was full of rubbish and a few 'empty' spirit bottles could have been spirited away in there and 'lost' for weeks, but apparently he always had enough to make at least one daily glass of the most explosive cocktails imaginable – a little bit of whiskey, a bit of rum, a few drops of gin, a few of tia maria and so on.

Don the postman eventually became embroiled in the affairs of this establishment, working occasionally on a number of things, including the roof.

To be precise the Waterloo had several roofs, all of them high, some more than others and they all leaked. We all took to roof climbing and it was hair-raising. On one of the highest sections trouble down near the gutter could be reached by pushing a ladder out from a skylight. This my father had done a couple of years earlier with Ron hanging on to the top end of the ladder. It was dangerous but it was possible, whereas going up a ladder on the outside of the building was not possible. No one had ladders long enough.

My father's handiwork on that part of the roof was as efficient as most other things he did with a hammer and nails, and when the water started to run through the ceilings again, Don the postman volunteered to put in a few new slates.

He was also a part-time fireman and was therefore conscious of the danger and the need to take precautions. Even so he went upstairs that morning with Bob as his assistant!

Apparently the first thing Bob did was knock back his mid-morning medicine, and when they'd pushed the ladder through the skylight and had laid it down the roof, they attached it by a rope to the biggest thing in the room, the

144

bed.

I'm not sure what happened exactly, but I know Don went out onto the roof and clambered down to the bottom of the ladder, and Bob stayed put. I think holding the rope.

All went well for a few minutes with Don loosening the broken slates, but then with no warning at all, the ladder slid down the roof with a terrifying clatter and Don found himself coming to a halt several feet beyond the gutter, clinging on for dear life to a ladder with nothing beneath it but thin air.

Bob it seems, had decided to lie on the bed and have a sleep and it had suddenly shot across the room. It was on casters.

In time Don got back in through the skylight, to find Bob still asleep on the bed, but if the postman had fallen that would have been the end of him, and I've often wondered if there was something in the old place that knew the end was near, and as time crept by it was trying to take us with it.

We all had narrow escapes from a whole catalogue of disasters, several of us fell through floors, especially where we'd 'borrowed' the floorboards, and several received head injuries from huge lumps of falling plaster from the ceiling. They used to fall like bombs. My father fell off one of the lower parts of the roof and survived, and my mother survived a serious attack of food poisoning.

Amazingly she picked it up at someone else's hotel which we were all very pleased about, but in fact, I think all of us who stayed until the end, came close one way or another to a bizarre and indelible demise.

One night we nearly all drowned in a sea of sausage and mash. The sixties provided a great time for slot machines. Or not such a great time for slot machines, depending on how you look at it.

It was my mother's idea to buy this latest culinary wonder of the age. Everyone said it was a daft idea but she thought it was a wonderful idea. According to the instructions all you had to do was hold a plate under the chute, stick two bob in the slot, press a button and hey presto, out would plop a nice steaming hot portion of sausage and mash.

I'm afraid we had a lot of slot machines. My mother loved them. She fancied herself as a test pilot I think, and was always the first to try them out. The fruit machines were her favourite, and if you heard an enormous cheer go up in the middle of the singing, you knew she'd won the jackpot yet again.

We had all sorts of slot machines including one that was always in the front bar, in a very prominent position because of its importance. It told you if you were too drunk to drive safely. You put a three-penny bit in at the top and if you couldn't press a button quick enough to stop it dropping to the bottom, you were over the limit. Not that there was a limit in those days.

I can't remember exactly how the sausage and mash machine worked, but it was probably on the line of our soft ice cream machine, with drums of powder being mixed with water or milk powder. However, what is certain is that when we all gathered in a rather confined space to watch my mother drop the first coin in, it belched loudly and instantly spewed forth a steaming torrent of sausage and mash at such a terrific rate that, try desperately as we did, we couldn't stop it! It gushed out like wet concrete flowing from the back of a ready mix lorry, and by the time Dai and I had managed to drag the machine away from the wall and switch it off, we were covered in the stuff. We looked like Bob when we'd pulled him from the wet concrete.

It made a terrible mess. It covered everything especially the floor of course, and it immediately set hard like a coating of china clay, with sausages sticking out of it.

The machine went back and was never seen again.

The biggest problem though with the Waterloo was definitely the roof, and always it posed the greatest danger.

It wasn't only the slates of course that were cracked and leaking, the chimneys too were in a bad state, and up on that complicated roof there were several areas that could only be reached from windows, and my father took once to venturing out completely unaided. I remember looking up and seeing him crawling on his hands and knees across a plank that he'd pushed out of a window in the tower to rest on a chimney pot about 12 feet away. He was slowly crawling along with his pipe jammed between his teeth like 'Popeye the Sailorman' and if he'd fallen there, that would have been his last fall.

One day however, a miracle happened. Someone else volunteered to do the roof.

It was a nice Spring morning just a few days before Easter. Bob came to look after the pumps while I went for a cup of coffee. I found my father in the snack bar and he told me of the marvellous news.

"They're builders from Blaenau I think," he said. "They came in the bar this morning saying they'd lost a job they were ready to start, and would I like them to have a look at the roof."

My father told them they didn't need to look at it. "Just go up and mend it," he said, and when he told them exactly what he wanted doing, they agreed on a very reasonable price, chicken feed in fact, even by our standards.

Later that morning they were back to weigh the place up. There were four of them weighing up the problems of getting ladders up from here to there, and there to there and so on, and the plan they came up with had all the hallmarks of the professional builder.

With the roof being so high, they planned to launch their ladders from an elevated position, going up through the loft of the old pre-war kitchen behind the bar where Bob hid his cocktails, and although of course that meant making a hole in the roof out there, it was still a good idea because the old place was so dilapidated it just wasn't going to matter and furthermore, the slates they removed would be used to mend broken slates up on the main roof.

It was quite ingenious really and they spent the day in preparation. They started to take the slates off the old kitchen roof and by the end of the afternoon they were all neatly stacked in rows.

As they went they said they'd be back tomorrow with the ladders.

That night we had an attempted break in.

The dogs woke me and by the fury of their barking I knew it was a truncheon job. Under the bed I kept a handy chair leg.

The dogs we had by this period were extremely good house dogs and at night they slept in the bar guarding the stock. One was Toby, a young black Labrador and the other was a skinny black and white mongrel by the name of Bute. He was the boss. A more savage dog when roused I hope never to meet, and they were practically tearing down the door that led to the old kitchen.

Bute was absolutely furious and as soon as I unbolted the door they flew through it, and I honestly think they would have ripped any burglars to bits, but there was no one in sight.

There was a long passage that had to be searched by torch-light leading off into various rooms full of junk, but there was no sign of anybody, and when my father came down he reckoned it must have been a false alarm, but the dogs didn't agree.

Bute was tearing up and down with his orange eyes glaring like hot embers. He was both growling and drooling at the same time, and his fangs gleamed like ivory daggers, but we never found a sign of *anyone.*

The dogs were shut in the bar again and we went back to bed, and it wasn't until the next morning that it all became clear.

The first thing was that the 'builders' didn't turn up.

The second thing was that Bob discovered a hole in the ceiling out in the old kitchens. In the dark we hadn't noticed it high up in the corner, and of course it provided a way in, exactly where the so-called builders had been making their hole in the slates.

"Indeed yes," the sergeant said, stroking his chin. "It's all they were after you see. They were making a way down, not up, they were making a way into your bar."

It was perfectly obvious that's all they were doing; they

weren't going to repair the roof at all, but the police didn't catch up with them. My father had no idea who they were, he'd taken them completely on trust and nothing in writing, no addresses, no names, and of course we never saw them again, but with Easter coming there were rich pickings in that bar, and especially in the store cupboard. There must have been hundreds and hundreds of pounds worth of spirits and cigarettes locked away in there, thousands of pounds worth of today's prices, but Bute and Toby weren't going to let anybody near it after closing time.

So many places were burgled every summer in that village and we had our share of attempted break-ins, but those two dogs defeated them every time.

There was a night though when they disappeared. I thought they must have been lured away by someone who'd be back later that night, but no one else thought so.

It was well into the tourist season, the place was stocked up to the ceiling and I reckoned we were sitting ducks without the early warning system.

"Give them another shout," my father said as he was cleaning up in the snack bar and I did, but it was to no avail. I gave them another shout after I'd finished washing the glasses too, but that was no good either. My voice echoed out across the car park and bounced back off the forest, but there was no trace of them.

They'd been around as usual earlier in the evening, leaping for beer mats, scrounging for crisps, and drinking from the slop trays under the beer pumps, but for the first time ever they'd gone out and disappeared before closing time.

Earlier, when at last the singing had come to an end, and the crowds were drifting away, old Bob had said "Where'rz dogsz Nox?" but I hadn't taken much notice at the time. "Perhaps they've got shut in the toilets," my mother suggested, but a quick search revealed everything but dogs, and bolting all the doors my father said they'd just have to stay out for the night.

"But supposing someone's lured them into a car or a van or something with a couple of bones?" I remember saying.

"Well what do you expect me to do about it?" my father said picking up the sackful of money that he always took to bed with him.

I argued that eliminating the dogs was the most sensible thing anyone could do who wanted a crack at breaking in.

"I bet someone will try and break in tonight," I said.

"Well I'm going to bed," my father said.

"But anyone could break in tonight and we'd never know."

"No one's going to break in," he said irritably. "Those dogs will be sitting on the doorstep in the morning."

"I bet they're locked up somewhere."

"Well I'm going to bed."

"Well I'm staying down here," I said realising as soon as I'd said it, that this was how he always got me to volunteer for things; and loosening my tie I threw some cushions on the floor and settled down to sleep by the fire.

It was a sleepless couple of hours and that's all it took for the dogs to return. I awoke with them scratching and whining at the front door.

Unceremoniously I let them in and booted the pair of them into their place behind the bar, shut them in and went upstairs.

My room was very narrow. It wasn't very long either but it was extremely narrow, just wide enough for a single bed, and to stand in front of the wardrobe meant standing with my back almost against the wall, and feeling somewhat jaded I stood there pulling off my clothes and throwing them into the wardrobe until something made me stop abruptly.

I froze.

The wardrobe was wide open, and as there was a mirror on the inside of the door, I could see the wall very close behind me. Just behind my head, was a big black 'thing' clinging to the wall.

It was the spider! I spun round and *stared* at it. It was enormous! Every bit as big as its reputation. So big it bore no resemblance to anything British, household, or harmless.

After a while, I recovered enough to get a pencil and I marked around it on the wall before it shot off! I've never seen a spider move so fast. It shot round and round that room like a motorbike on the wall of death.

I'd never minded about spiders until then, but that room just wasn't big enough for the two of us, he had to go, and I caught up with him after a while under the bed where he'd got a foot stuck in my badminton racquet. I pulled the racquet out covered in a load of fluff and putting a heavier tennis racquet on him to hold him down, I dropped him out of the window.

Grabbing the torch I watched him float down on a parachute of fluff and land in the grass outside the snack bar two storeys below.

For a while it didn't move and I wondered if it was alright. He was too magnificent to kill, but at the same time he was a threat to ones sanity if not actual life and limb. No one would sleep if they knew that thing was on the prowl.

I ducked back in and looked at the marks on the wall. I took a five pound note off the bedside table and held it to the pencil marks. It fitted almost exactly. The 'thing' whatever it was, had almost been the size of a five pound note, and they were a bit bigger in those days.

I shone the torch down onto the grass again. It had gone.

I shone the torch over the road and then back down the path alongside the building, and there it was. It was by an old trapdoor that dropped into one of the cellars.

It suddenly lurched forward and crawled underneath it. It was back.

ooooOooooo

No doubt his end came when the Waterloo was demolished and the old place came crashing down, and I expect he'd been there a lot longer than we had.

Soon after that encounter with the spider, in those last few months before my father died, I brought a young wife to the Waterloo. We turned one of the old stables into a cottage, yes the one all my mates had been sprawling in, but I don't think I told her that. She made it beautiful though, really beautiful, but it's all gone now. Both my parents are dead, old Bob too and most of the others. Like the tourists we at the Waterloo also bounced off the window of village life without leaving a mark, and as you pass through Betws-y-Coed today, you'd never know that it had all happened, but it did.

Wonderful days, wonderful people.